Shanawdithit's People

The Archaeology of the Beothuks

Ralph T. Pastore

Published by Atlantic Archaeology Ltd.
226 Mt. Scio Road
St. John's, Newfoundland
A1B 4L5
© 1992 Atlantic Archaeology Ltd.
ISBN 0-929048-02-4

Distributed by Breakwater Books
100 Water Street
P.O. Box 2188
St. John's, Newfoundland
A1E 6E6

All rights reserved. No part of this publication may be reproduced, stored in a retrieval system or transmitted in any form or by any means, electronic, mechanical, photocpoying, recording or otherwise, without the prior permisssion of Atlantic Archaeology Ltd.

Cover: Last remnants of the Beothuks bear the body of Demasduit, or Mary March, who died in 1820, across Red Indian Lake to her final resting place.
From the film *Finding Mary March*, courtesy of Ken Pittman, Red Ochre productions; cinematographer Michael Jones

CONTENTS

THE PREHISTORY OF THE BEOTHUKS 1

BEOTHUK CULTURE 13

THE BEOTHUK SITE AT BOYD'S COVE 27

THE EXTINCTION OF THE BEOTHUKS 47

ACKNOWLEDGEMENTS 74

The Prehistory of the Beothuks

For years the Beothuks, the aboriginal inhabitants of the Island of Newfoundland, were regarded as a mysterious people who shrank from contact with Europeans and whose last member, Shanawdithit, died in 1829. In the past twenty years, discoveries made by archaeologists, historians, and linguists have helped to lift much of the mystery from these people, but the tragedy of their demise remains. The extinction of an entire people is a terrible thing, and it requires us to try to to understand what happened. Often, that process of understanding is a difficult one. It may be easy to accept

Only known portrait of a Beothuk depicts Demasduit, or Mary March, painted in 1819 by Lady Hamilton, wife of the then governor of Newfoundland. Demasduit died, perhaps from tuberculosis, within a year of her capture.

Courtesy of the National Archives of Canada.

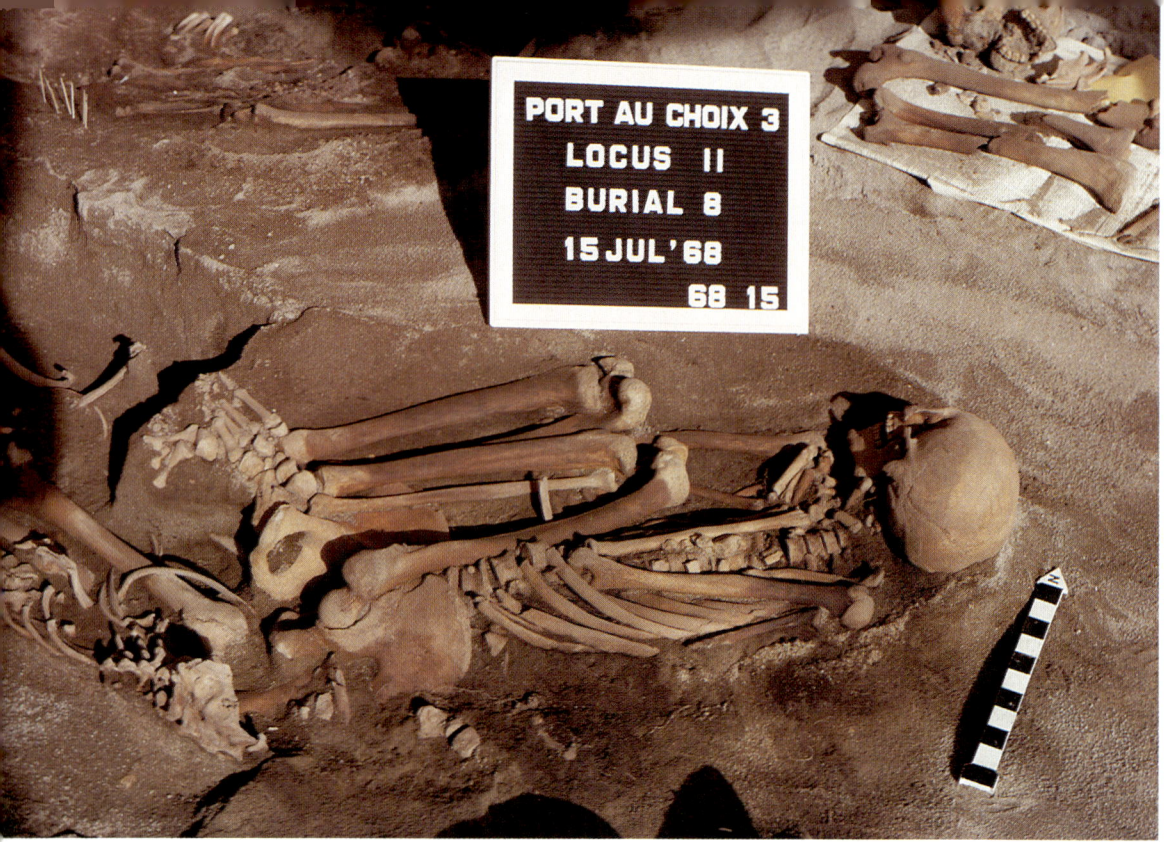

Excavated remains of an individual of the Maritime Archaic tradition—the people who first occupied the Island of Newfoundland.

the simple explanation that the ancestors of today's Newfoundlanders were criminals who slaughtered the Beothuks 'for fun' as one writer expressed it. But the past is seldom that simple, and it is not enough to accept the easy answer that early Newfoundland settlers were more cruel and more violent than other Europeans in other parts of Canada who did not exterminate the Native peoples whose lands they also took.

Although, as we will see, we now have answers to what happened to the Beothuks and why it happened, we still cannot be certain of the origins of the Beothuks. The first inhabitants of the Island of Newfoundland were a people belonging to what archaeologists refer to as the Maritime Archaic tradition. In this sense, the term tradition refers to a way of life stretching over a long period of time and found in a specific area— in this case the coastal region from New Brunswick to northern Labrador. Much of what we know about these people is the result of work done at sites such as Port au Choix. Here, some 53 burials revealed a culture heavily oriented toward exploiting the resources of the sea: the seals, fish, birds, and shellfish of Newfoundland's coasts. Although this pattern of reliance upon food from the sea would occur for all of Newfoundland's Native peoples, including the Beothuks, we cannot trace Beothuk ancestry directly back to the Maritime Archaic people. The Maritime Archaic Indians appear to have come to Newfoundland from the mainland some time before about 5,000 years ago, and at some time after about 3,500 years ago they either became extinct, or their numbers dwindled so low that they have not been detected by archaeologists.

The island was then occupied by an early Palaeo-Eskimo (palaeo = old) people sometimes known as the Groswater people. They were part of a widely-spread, but thinly populated, culture which extended over much of the eastern Canadian arctic. Their occupancy of the island lasted from about 2,700 years ago until about 2,100 years before present. These early Palaeo-Eskimo people were succeeded by a later Palaeo-Eskimo people usually referred to by archaeologists as the Dorset Eskimo. Their distinctive tools have been found almost everywhere on the island, and they may have been the most numerous of all of Newfoundland's prehistoric peoples. They too, became extinct, in their case sometime before about A.D. 800.

Exquisite stone tools characterize both early Palaeo-Eskimo (bottom) and Dorset Eskimo (top) cultures. Shown here, from left to right, are graving tools used to carve bone and antler, end blades used to tip harpoons and knives used for cutting meat and other substances.

Diagram illustrates the time of year when Newfoundland's food resources were available. The thickened portion of the horizontal line indicates when the resource was most abundant; dotted lines indicate that the resource was only marginally available. The chart shows that during some seasons people may have had to depend on stored foods.

This pattern of repeated extinction is very clear, and it has a bearing on what later happened to the Beothuks. All of the peoples we have looked at were heavily dependent upon the sea. Such resources as salmon, caplin, smelt, harp seals, and others have in common the fact that they arrive in enormous numbers at specific times of the year, usually on a regular basis. Ordinarily they supplied an abundance of food for the bands of prehistoric hunters and gatherers who harvested them. The problem, however, is that on a very few occasions these normally abundant resources either failed to arrive, or arrived in the wrong places, or in numbers much smaller than expected. When this sort of thing happened on the mainland, there were other animal stocks to which the hunters could turn—and in some cases even plants that could supply  the needed food. Newfoundland, however, was different in that while the resources of the coastline were usually quite plentiful, those of the interior were not. The most

Caribou, shown here in their winter coats, were often killed by the Beothuks as the animals crossed stretches of water during their fall migration. Meat was stored by freezing and drying to last through the harsh winter months.

Courtesy of Newfoundland and Labrador Environment and Lands, Wildlife Division.

Harp seals, such as this one shown on the ice off Newfoundland, still arrive by the millions each spring along the Newfoundland coasts. They were an important food source for all of the Native peoples to occupy the island.

Courtesy of Chesley Sanger.

important food of the interior upon which Newfoundland's aboriginal peoples depended was the caribou, a migratory animal which moves between feeding and calving grounds in huge herds. Unfortunately for prehistoric hunters, caribou are notorious for their unpredictability. Their usual migration patterns can change as a result of sleet storms, prevailing winds and other factors not completely understood. When this happens the result can be tragic, as was the case with a Naskapi band in northern Quebec-Labrador who, about 1916, failed to find the caribou herd that had been the mainstay of their diet for generations. When they arrived on the coast they were starving, and it is possible that the band would have died out had it not been for the help given them by the Hudson's Bay Company.

In the prehistoric period, however, the long-term survival of these mainland subarctic hunting bands depended on the taking of a variety of game at precise times of the year. If the caribou hunt failed in the fall, or if offshore winds prevented access to the harp seal herds at the end of winter, the hunters would be forced to fall back on emergency species such as porcupine, beaver, whitefish and others. Newfoundland, on the other hand, is remarkably deficient in these 'fall-back' species. There were no porcupine or whitefish on the island, and beaver populations were perhaps half the size of their mainland counterparts. Newfoundland's lakes and ponds have many fewer fish, both in terms of number of species and in total biomass. This scarcity extends to land animals as well, which is why Newfoundlanders decided to import moose and varying hare to the island in the nineteenth century—both of which prospered because they filled unoccupied niches of the island's ecosystem. There was room for these new species in Newfoundland because many of the less mobile prey species on the mainland had failed to migrate to the island. Newfoundland's soil was scraped off by the last glaciers, and because of the island's cool maritime climate, there was a very slow buildup of soil after the glaciers began to recede some 12,000-13,000 years ago. These conditions created a relatively barren island whose small human populations have always been, because of the nature of its resources, particularly vulnerable to extinction.

The beaver—the only major land animal besides caribou that provided food for Newfoundland's aboriginal peoples—may not have been present in large enough numbers to replace other meat sources in times of hardship.

Courtesy of Newfoundland and Labrador Environment and Lands, Wildlife Division.

Inspector Island, an important prehistoric and historic Beothuk site in eastern Notre Dame Bay, is typical of many Newfoundland Indian sites. It is protected from prevailing winds, has a sandy beach where canoes could have been drawn up and a nearby source of fresh water. As shown by the potato beds near the centre, the site was later occupied by Europeans.

The limitations of those resources, archaeologists believe, have meant that for most of the time, the island has been occupied by only one culture at a time. This is because, although the island's area is enormous, there is a limited number of places where prehistoric human settlements have existed. On the coast, such places often have a good beach upon which to draw up fragile vessels, fresh water nearby, a dry campground, and most importantly, nearness to a reliable food supply. This is why so many Newfoundland sites are multi-component in nature; that is, over time a succession of people lived and left their remains—called 'components' by archaeologists—at the site.

However, there is increasing evidence that sometime during the period, about A.D. 1 - A.D. 500, while Dorset Eskimos lived in Newfoundland, an Indian group from across the Strait of Belle Isle began to populate the island. This marks the beginning on the island of the so-called 'Recent Indian' period which ended with the extinction of the Beothuks. These first Recent Indians were almost certainly descended from Maritime Archaic peoples, but that succession seems to have occurred on the mainland, probably in the southern Quebec-Labrador region, rather than on the island. Little is known about the earliest of these Recent Indians to come to Newfoundland, but archaeologists have recognized the emergence, by about A.D. 1000, of what has been called the Beaches complex. The word 'complex' refers to the distinctive tools and other remains left behind by a people whose origins, duration, and geographical extent are poorly understood. For example, we know that the Beaches people made side-notched projectile points, linear flakes (easily made, roughly rectangular flakes that might have been used like disposable pocket knives), and largish, lanceolate 'bifaces' (tools chipped on both sides), which might have been used as all-purpose cutting and chopping tools. Many of these artifacts are made from a stone called rhyolite—a material easily obtainable in many parts of the island. At present we have one date of A.D. 960

Projectile points from the 'Beaches complex', thought to represent the prehistoric ancestors of the Beothuks, date to about A.D. 1000. The largest is 5.5cm long; the points may have been used to tip arrows, lances or spears.

produced by radiocarbon dating charcoal from a campfire made by Beaches people, but until we have more such dates, we cannot be sure exactly when this complex begins and ends. The complex itself was named after the Beaches site in northern Bonavista Bay, and this site, like most Recent Indian sites, is located in a protected 'inner' area of the bay. By contrast, Dorset Eskimo sites tend to be found on outer islands and exposed headlands. This pattern of Indian sites in sheltered inner areas and Dorset sites in exposed outer areas suggests that the Dorset people may have become somewhat more specialized in their hunting than the Indian peoples with whom they shared the island. While the Dorset people may have concentrated on marine resources, particularly the migratory harp seal herds, their Indian neighbours may have had a somewhat more generalized strategy that was more dependent on a wider variety of both sea and land resources. If the Dorset people relied more exclusively on the harp seal, a failure of the harp seal herd to arrive might have resulted in their extinction.

When the Dorset people became extinct, the Beaches people seem to have expanded their range and perhaps increased in number. By about A.D. 1200 their descendants were making many of their stone tools out of fine-grained blue-green and grey-green cherts. The material and style of these artifacts are similar to, but sufficiently different from, what came before, that archaeologists have called this new pattern of tools and materials the Little Passage complex. It was named after the Little Passage site on Newfoundland's south coast where it was first discovered by archaeologist Gerald Penney. These projectile points are noticeably smaller than those of the preceding Beaches complex, and it is possible that their appearance is an indication that the Little Passage people had adopted the bow and arrow and were using these little points as arrowheads.

Fist-sized 'core' of grey-green chert shows scars left when flakes used to make smaller tools and weapons were removed by striking the core with a stone hammer. The stone is typical of the material favoured by people of the prehistoric Little Passage complex.

Arrowpoints or harpoon end blades from Newfoundland's Little Passage complex date from a few centuries prior to contact with Europeans. Although made from different raw materials, examples from Labrador identical in form and size (about three centimetres in length) suggest continued contact across the Strait of Belle Isle.

Although the Little Passage tools are different from those of the Beaches people, the Little Passage sites are also often found in sheltered, inner regions of the coast.

As yet, we know little about the Little Passage people other than what can be gleaned from their stone tools, but even that has led to some exciting tentative conclusions. Although not made from the same raw material, these tools are very similar in appearance to tools that were made on the Quebec-Labrador coast. On both sides of the Strait of Belle Isle, the projectile points made by these people gradually change from larger side-notched points to the tiny stemmed points made by the historic Beothuks. This is one of the most important reasons why many archaeologists believe that the Little Passage people were the direct ancestors of the Beothuks. In fact, were it not for the arrival of Europeans to Newfoundland there would be no sharp dividing line between the Little Passage people and the Beothuks. When Europeans came to Newfoundland, however, the pace of cultural change quickened and Newfoundland's Indians can then be called the Beothuks.

The arrival of Europeans should not distract us from the fact that the stone tool technologies of the inhabitants of the island and those of southern coastal Quebec-Labrador were very similar. This suggests a long standing relationship over time which allows

Gradual changes in style and size mark the evolution of Newfoundland Indian projectile points. The specimen on the lower left may date to about A.D. 1000-1100, while the tiny arrowpoint at the upper right was made by Beothuks in the late seventeenth or early eighteenth century.

archaeologists to speak of a Recent Indian tradition extending from almost two thousand years ago to the historic Beothuks and perhaps to the Innu of Quebec-Labrador. It is quite possible, therefore, that the Naskapi-Montagnais are the surviving relatives of the Beothuks. The linguist, John Hewson, for example, has suggested that the Beothuk spoke a variation of Central Algonkian, as do the Naskapi-Montagnais, unlike the Micmac of Nova Scotia whose language belongs to the Eastern Algonkian sub-group. The possibility of a relationship between the Indians of Newfoundland and those of Labrador is strengthened by the account of the last of the Beothuks who said that the Beothuks were on very good terms with the Montagnais—as one would expect of two closely-related peoples.

Certainly it is true that in prehistoric times there was contact between Recent Indian groups on the island and those in Labrador. Tools from Newfoundland are sometimes made of Ramah chert, an attractive translucent chert found only in northern Labrador, while some Recent Indian tools from southern Quebec-Labrador are made from cherts found on the west coast of the Island of Newfoundland. Travel across the Strait of Belle Isle might have been easier in prehistoric times, but the arrival of Europeans, and then Inuit, in the Strait seems to have made communication more difficult between the Indians of Newfoundland and those of Labrador.

Beothuk Culture

When the first Europeans arrived in Newfoundland they found a hunting and gathering people who were living in small groups. The total number of those groups is not known, however, and until a great deal more archaeological work is done, we will not be able to arrive at a firm estimate of the total Beothuk population on the island—and we should remember that there is a good possibility that there was an equally unknown number of Beothuks on the other side of the Strait of Belle Isle in Quebec-Labrador. Scholarly estimates for the number of Beothuks on the island when the first European stepped ashore vary from 500 to 2,000. Given the relatively small number of Little Passage (prehistoric Beothuk) sites, and the limitations of the Newfoundland environment, it seems reasonable to accept a population estimate closer to the lower end of this range.

Detail from John Cartwright's 'A Sketch of the River Exploits...' shows Beothuk houses and canoes. Although Cartwright failed to contact any Beothuks during his trip in 1768 he did visit Beothuk villages, perhaps hastily abandoned at the arrival of Europeans.

Courtesy of the Newfoundland Museum.

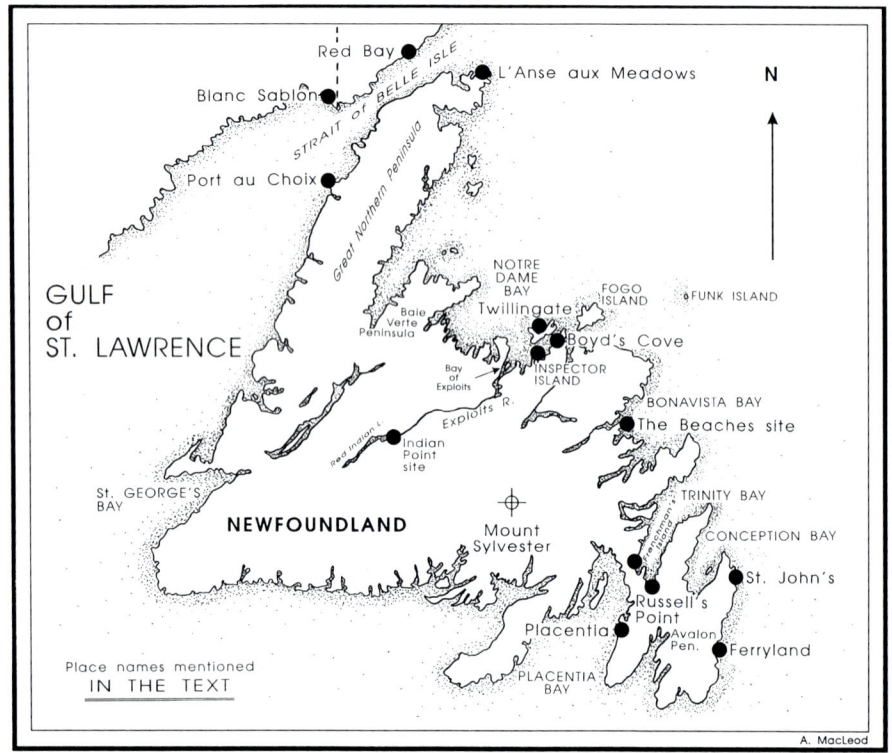

Map of Newfoundland shows places mentioned in the text. Archaeologists believe that the major regions of the island, such as Bonavista Bay, Trinity-Placentia Bay and so forth may each have supported a band or two of Beothuks.

Judging by the evidence from prehistoric Beothuk sites, as well as what we know from comparable societies around the world, it is clear that the Beothuks lived in what archaeologists call a band society. Such a society consists, for the most part, of small groups, often no more that 35-50 individuals. When the master and crew of the Bristol ship, the *Grace*, for example, went ashore in St. George's Bay in 1594, they saw 'the tracks of the feete of some fortie or fiftie men, women and children'—and this may well have been typical for a band of the period. By the early part of the nineteenth century, when the remnants of the Beothuks were clustered together at Red Indian Lake in the interior of the island, the size of the group might have been larger.

Throughout their history these bands would not have had chiefs, but there would have been individuals who, because of their wisdom, skill, and experience would have had more influence than other band members. Decisions, however, would be the result of compromise and consensus; no one person in a band society could order another to do anything. Another characteristic of band society is that its members acquire, rather than inherit, status. That is, their position in society is not due to their family's prestige, but because they have earned the respect of other members of their society—as particularly able hunters, for example.

Beothuk society may well have consisted of such bands of perhaps a half dozen related families. If the Beothuks resembled other hunting and gathering band-level societies, we would expect that a number of these bands would congregate at a certain time of year when and where resources would be unusually abundant—at an interior caribou kill site, for example—or at a place along the coast where a large harp seal kill would be assured. Here, the meeting of a number of bands would allow people to choose marriage partners from other bands. Such congregations may also have been the occasion for trade in things like stone tools, furs, and canoes.

Indian Brook not only provided fresh water for the occupants of the Boyd's Cove site, but was the scene of a major smelt run. The yellowish material in the stream is smelt eggs, deposited during the first two weeks of May. The Beothuks timed their seasonal movements very precisely to take advantage of such specific resources.

The time of year when a number of bands could gather would have been determined by the availability of food. In fact, a combination of factors, of which food would have been the most important, set the schedule of Beothuk movements throughout the year. Hunting and gathering peoples are sometimes described as following a nomadic way of life, but this does not mean that bands wandered randomly over the landscape. Quite the contrary, the movements of hunting bands were usually precisely scheduled according to the group's needs. A prehistoric Beothuk band, for example, would have to position itself so that it could take harp seals in the early spring, migratory sea birds a bit later, salmon, capelin and smelt in the early summer, inshore fish throughout the warmer months, and caribou in the fall when the animals began to move

Stone tools used by Little Passage complex people include flaked knives (left) used for cutting and chopping, scrapers (centre) used to remove fat from hides and linear or 'blade-like' flakes (right) that were easily made, disposable cutting tools.

prior to moving to their winter feeding grounds. As well as the quest for food, Beothuks would have also had to time their movements so as to be in the right places at right times to pick up supplies of chert to make stone tools, birch bark to make canoes and containers, iron pyrites (which were used to start fires), red ochre for decoration, and so forth. This meant that the Beothuks had an intimate knowledge of their country. The prehistoric Beothuks who lived in Notre Dame Bay, for example, made most of their tools from fine-grained, blue-green and grey-green cherts that geologists tell us are most likely chipped from boulders brought down by glaciers thousands of years ago. Today, one can travel by boat and foot for months, as some archaeologists have, and not find such boulders. Their use as raw material for Beothuk tools drives home the point that the territories of hunting peoples were as familiar to them as the local neighbourhoods of modern urban dwellers are to them. Similarly, in eastern Notre Dame Bay there is only one place in the region where smelt spawn. That site shows a long history of repeated prehistoric occupations, and would have been as well known to the Beothuk band who camped there as a summer house would be to its modern family's owners.

This detailed knowledge of the landscape was paralleled by an equally detailed understanding of the habits of animals. It was necessary to know where and when flatfish could be speared, how to deal with the occasional polar bear that

Beothuk projectile point (left) was carefully crafted by hammering and grinding a European nail. It was made by the people who lived at Boyd's Cove and probably served as an arrowpoint. Two Beothuk harpoons are made from antler; the example at the right is tipped with an iron end blade. The harpoons were designed to twist, or 'toggle', in the wound, preventing the animal's escape.

Courtesy of the Newfoundland Museum.

blundered into camp, what eggs could be gathered in May, and an immense quantity of other information needed to stay alive.

To take advantage of the variety of animal species found in Newfoundland and its coastal waters, the Beothuks developed an efficient hunting technology. For seals, the Beothuks used a sophisticated toggling harpoon. The harpoon itself was made of bone and tipped with a stone end blade (replaced by iron after the arrival of Europeans). It had a hollow socket into which a bone foreshaft was fitted. Bone was used because a thin piece of bone is much stronger than a wooden shaft of comparable thickness. The bone foreshaft would have been inserted into a much larger wooden shaft held by the harpooner. The harpoon head itself was secured to a line, and would detach from the shaft when driven into a seal. In the wound, the barbs, or shoulders, of the harpoon would cause it to 'toggle,' or twist, so that the prey would remain secure. (It is interesting to note that European whalers did not adopt toggling harpoons until the nineteenth century after hundreds of years of whaling.) Other animals like caribou and beaver were killed with lances and bows and arrows. Once killed, the animals were butchered with stone knives and sharp stone flakes—as sharp, in fact, as a modern scalpel. Fat was scraped from the hides with stone scrapers and the skins were then made into clothing and containers.

17

After the Beothuks had access to European materials—often pilfered from European fishermen and fur trappers—iron was substituted for stone. Nails were fashioned into sharp arrow points, and trap parts were hammered into large deer spears. Nails with their shafts flattened and pieces of cast iron may have also been substituted for stone and used as hide scrapers.

While the Beothuks readily replaced stone with iron as a raw material for their cutting and piercing tools, they retained traditional materials for many other purposes, such as the skins used to make containers for food. In fact, the historically-known Beothuks had very sophisticated methods for storing food and it is likely that prehistoric Beothuks did as well. Indeed, given the fact that for some periods of the year there were few alternatives to the usual prey—caribou or seal—it may have been just as necessary to preserve food in the prehistoric period as it was in the historic era. Meat was sometimes preserved by placing it inside skin bags filled with seal oil. Such treatment might not have made it very good to taste, but it would have lasted for months. One observer also reported that the Beothuks dried and powdered egg yolks and kept them in birch bark vessels. Another writer described a similar food produced by making '…a kind of a cake made of eggs baked in the sun, and a sort of pudding stuffed in a gut and composed of seals fat, livers, eggs, and other ingredients.'

No examples of prehistoric Beothuk clothing have survived, and thus what we know about this aspect of their life must be based on historical reports and museum specimens of clothing worn by historic Beothuks. The favoured material for that clothing was

Beothuk child's moccasin was found in a grave in western Notre Dame Bay in 1886.

Courtesy of the Newfoundland Museum.

caribou skins which, because of their hollow hair, are lightweight and extremely warm. Both men and women wore long, loose cloaks, and in colder weather, leggings, moccasins, sealskin hats, arm coverings and mittens could be added. Our knowledge of Beothuk appearance is based partially on the accounts of Europeans, such as the would-be settler, John Guy, who attempted to plant a colony in Conception Bay in 1610. He described their appearance in these words:

Lightweight, tough and portable bark containers were used in place of pottery by the Beothuks.

Courtesy of the Mary March Regional Museum.

[They are] of a reasonable stature, of an ordinary middle size, they goe bare-headed, wearing their hair somewhat long but round: they have no beards; behind they have a great locke of haire platted with feathers like a hawke's lure, with a feather in it standing upright by the crowne of the head and a small lock platted before, a short gown made of stags' skins, the furre innermost, that raune down to the middle of their legges, with sleeves to the middle of their arme, and a bever skin about their necke, was all their apparell, save that one of them had shooes and mittens, so that all went bare-legged and most bare-foote. They are full-eyed, of a blacke colour; the colour of their hair was divers, some blacke some browne, and some yellow [possibly stained with yellow ochre?], and their faces something flat and broad, red with oker, as all their apparell is, and the rest of their body: they are broad breasted and bould and stand very upright.

For travelling, the Beothuks relied on a superbly designed canoe. It was made of a light wooden frame covered over with birch bark, sewn together with spruce roots, and waterproofed with spruce gum. These canoes ranged from perhaps 12 to 22 feet in length, and were apparently capable of making voyages as far out as the Funk Islands, a distance of some 57 kilometres from the main part of the island. They were built with a high bow and stern, and a 'hogged sheer'—a high rise in the central portions of the sides of the canoe—all of which resulted in a canoe able to cope with the waves and swells so often encountered off Newfoundland's coasts. In winter, the Beothuks travelled on snowshoes made of a wooden framework over which was

Beothuk canoes, similar to this replica, were capable of travelling considerable distance in the open sea.

Courtesy of Exploits Valley Tourism Association.

stretched a network of skin strips. This enabled Beothuk hunters to travel over the deep, soft drifts characteristic of central Newfoundland's winters.

This picture of Beothuk travel is based on what we know from the historic period; we have no direct knowledge of prehistoric Beothuk canoes or snowshoes. Much the same is true for our understanding of Beothuk housing.

To date, we have found no evidence of prehistoric Beothuk, or Little Passage, structures. All that have been found are small hearths—the remains of campfires—around which archaeologists have reported clusters of tools, the debris of stone tool making, and, occasionally, animal bones. From this evidence, we believe that prehistoric Beothuks lived in temporary shelters, perhaps skin or bark tents stretched over a light framework of poles. Such dwellings would have left little, if any, impression in the shallow soils of Newfoundland.

The Little Passage dwellings, in fact, may have resembled one of the types of houses that the Beothuks built—the temporary conical structures that a number of Europeans observed. In 1594, for example, Beothuk houses in St. George's Bay were reported as

Reconstructed wigwam at Indian Point, Red Indian Lake, consists of a framework of poles covered with bark. It may have been favoured for warm weather occupation.

being 'made of firre trees bound together in the top and set round like a Dovehouse, and covered with the barkes of firre trees.' John Guy also described these houses as 'nothing but poles set in round forme, meeting altogether aloft, which they cover with Deere skins; they are about ten foot broad, and in the middle they make their fire: one of them was covered with a saile, which they had gotten from some Christian [European].'

When Europeans came to Newfoundland, the Beothuks were still using such structures, but sometime after the initial contact, the Beothuks had begun to build much more substantial dwellings. We do not yet understand how Beothuk housing changed over time, but the accounts of a number of Europeans coupled with recent discoveries at sites in Notre Dame Bay have given us a rough idea of what seems to have happened. At some point after about A.D. 1500 the Beothuks began to build substantial pit houses as well as temporary living structures. Excavations at two Beothuk sites inhabited in the late seventeenth/early eighteenth centuries have revealed pit houses built in the following manner: the house builders began by digging a shallow depression, about five to six metres in diameter, and erecting a wigwam in the interior. The wig-

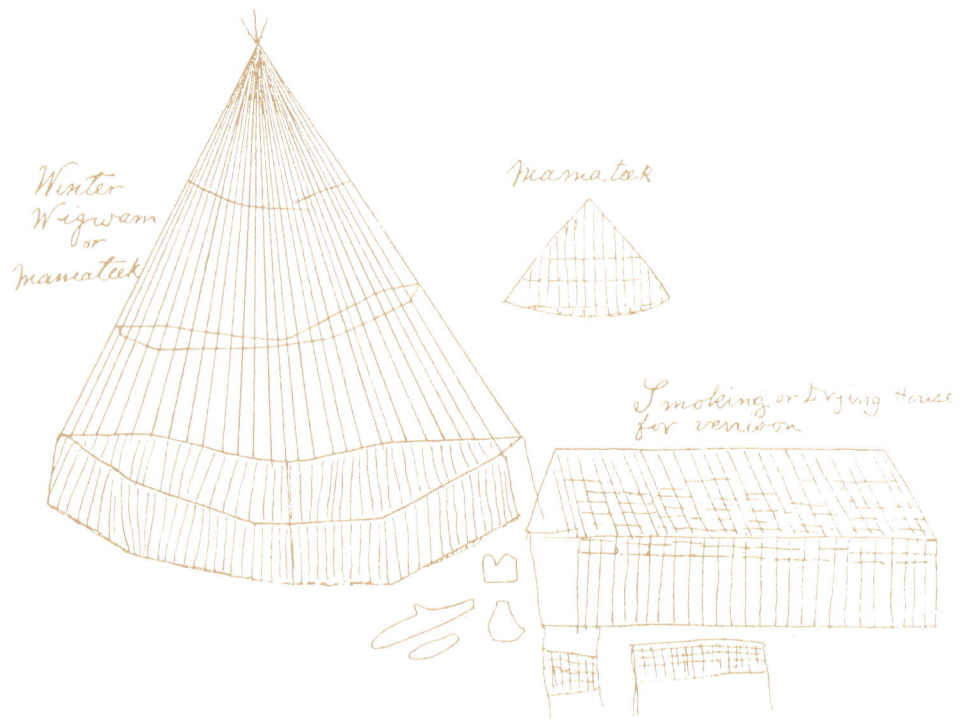

Sketch of a winter wigwam (left), a conical summer wigwam (centre and a smoking or drying house (right) was made by Shanawdithit, last known Beothuk woman before her death in 1829.

Courtesy of the Newfoundland Museum.

wam was constructed by forcing poles into the soil or into shallow holes dug for them. These posts may have supported horizontal stringers, or poles upon which rested other poles serving as rafters. The use of these horizontal stringers would have resulted in houses which would have appeared multi-sided, or 'sub-circular.' The rafters angled inward from these stringers, and may have been fastened with spruce roots and in some cases may have been braced by interior supports. The entire structure would have been roofed over with a waterproof covering of over-lapping sheets of bark. Other poles were placed against the outside of that bark roof, and the bases of those poles were buried in earthen walls made from the soil excavated from the house interior. When piled around the outside of the house, the earthen walls would have been very effective insulation against the winter's cold.

By the late eighteenth or early nineteenth century, Europeans who saw Beothuk camps described very solid structures, some square, others octagonal, built of squared logs, and, in one instance, with a double wall with deerskins lining the space between the two walls. These dwellings were built at a time when the Beothuks were spending the period from September to May in the interior of the island hiding away from hostile fishermen and furriers, and it is tempting to speculate that this enforced residence for so long in the interior, coupled with a need to conserve energy (because of a lack of food) made the construction of such substantial buildings necessary.

The trend toward more substantial dwellings was probably only exaggerated by the need to spend so much time in the interior. This trend may have begun with the availability of European materials that occurred soon after contact. Those European goods may have brought changes that allowed or compelled the Beothuks to invest more time and energy in the building of substantial pit houses rather than relatively flimsy temporary structures. The substitution of iron for stone or bone, for example, might have resulted in a more efficient technology. Superior harpoons, lances, and arrowheads would mean a higher success rate in the taking of animals which in turn might have lessened the need to move from one place to another. It is also possible that nearby supplies of iron from abandoned fishing premises might have reduced the need to travel to distant chert sources. Iron cutting and digging tools might also have made the building of pit houses easier than in prehistoric times.

The very presence of pit houses themselves hints at a greater degree of permanent residence, or 'sedentism' as archaeologists call it, but we have faunal evidence (evidence from animal remains) at one Beothuk site that also suggests a greater commitment to place. From Boyd's Cove, a site on the coast in Notre Dame Bay whose Beothuk occupation was sometime during the period about A.D. 1650 to 1720, an analysis of the bird, mammal, and fish bones suggests an occupation from at least April to November. There was no clear evidence for occupation during the coldest months of the year, but this may be the result of an inadequate sample. It may be that the Boyd's Cove inhabitants dispersed inland in the middle of the winter, but it is just as likely that they spent the entire year on the coast. Although Boyd's Cove is a coastal site, it is situated deep at the bottom of Notre Dame Bay in a sheltered location, and hunters from Boyd's Cove would not have to travel very far inland to hunt caribou and beaver in the winter.

Iron axes, such as these from Beothuk sites in central Newfoundland, replaced stone tools and may have made construction of substantial wigwams easier.

Courtesy of the Newfoundland Museum.

Archaeologists and historians of the Native peoples of the Atlantic Provinces used to believe that in both historic and prehistoric times, Indians lived on the coast in the warmer months in comparatively large camps and broke into small groups to hunt in the interior in the winter. We now know that this picture may well have been distorted by the arrival of Europeans. There is increasing archaeological evidence to indicate that in prehistoric times there was considerable variety in seasonal movements. In the Gulf of Maine, for example, archaeologist David Sanger has found that a site located on the coast did not necessarily mean that it was occupied only in the summer. There was evidence for year-round occupation at one site, and winter occupation at others. These prehistoric hunter-gatherers, in other words, were quite flexible, and their stay in a particular area was dependent on local conditions. It is quite possible that Beothuk use of the island was also more complex than a simple pattern of summers spent on the coast and winters in the interior.

Soon after European fishermen and explorers began coming to North America, however, they began to trade with Indians for furs. Because of winter storms, European vessels only arrived in the warmer months. On the other hand, furs were at their finest in the winter, and hence a pattern arose of Indians hunting in the interior in the winter for furs and camping on the coast to await Europeans in the summer. In some cases this may have fitted in with an older seasonal pattern, but in others it may have warped the older seasonal round.

We do not know the exact nature of the earliest contacts between Europeans and Beothuks, but it is doubtful if those contacts would have lasted very long. It is more likely that the usual encounter between visiting fishermen and Beothuks took the form of a brief meeting where a few furs were ex-

Fish hook (left) and chisel or 'spud' (right), obtained in trade or scavenged from abandoned fishing premises, were more effective and durable than bone or stone counterparts. The chisel or spud may have been used to break into frozen beaver lodges during winter months. Fish hooks were often straightened and used as awls.

changed for a few knives, some fish hooks, and perhaps an old kettle or two. We can be sure that the Beothuks found metal highly desirable. Although it is possible to produce stone tools with an edge sharper than steel, stone dulls very quickly and is much more brittle than iron. Iron edged tools are tough and can be easily resharpened. Throughout the world, whenever the opportunity has presented itself, people have replaced their stone tools with those made of iron.

Metal was not all that Native peoples wanted. They were also willing to trade furs for seemingly worthless items such as glass beads and scraps of copper and brass. Although Europeans of the time were amazed that they could exchange such trifles for valuable furs, we should remember that Europeans often purchased the very furs which Natives were actually wearing—the equivalent, perhaps, of trading our old clothes to aliens from outer space who had brought wondrous new materials with them. Not all European 'trifles' were equally valued, however. After considerable study of a number of northeastern Indian cultures, anthropologist George Hamell found that certain colours were possessed of deep spiritual meaning. This should not be surprising; even in our own society, white can be a symbol of purity, black a sign of mourning, and so on. For the Indians of the northeast, white and translucent colours embodied the concepts of goodness and spiritual power, which may be why white and translucent glass beads were highly valued. It may also explain why translucent Ramah chert from northern Labrador has been found in graves as far south as southern New England. Red appears to have been associated with life and health, and blue with the sky and with the powerful beings of the sky. It is surely no accident that Indians prized translucent and white beads, red beads and red cloth, as well as reddish copper and brass, and blue beads. Theories such as

Ramah chert, from which this stone tool was made, comes only from a small area in northern Labrador. Its presence in Newfoundland is evidence of prehistoric trade links between the people of Labrador and those on the Island of Newfoundland.

25

this may provide an insight into the nature of Beothuk religion, but the fact is that we know very little about Beothuk spiritual beliefs. However, every Indian hunter-gatherer religion about which we know something has a number of things in common. Such hunting peoples, for example, did not draw a sharp line between religious and ordinary behaviour. They did not, as we usually do, ignore the religious side of life for all but an hour a week. For Native hunter-gatherers, all life was a religious activity. The animals had to be treated with respect, and when killed, their remains had to be disposed of in ways that would not offend the spirit of the animal. Trade, too, was in part a spiritual activity, particularly in the early stages when that trade involved substances that were associated with a people's deeply held spiritual beliefs. The first Europeans who may have exchanged a few glass beads and scraps of cloth with a Beothuk for a few furs may have thought themselves engaging in a simple economic transaction, but we can be sure that this exchange was much more meaningful to the Beothuks.

Wooden figure was found with a child's burial in western Notre Dame Bay, may have been a plaything or may have had some religious significance. Since no Europeans ever lived with the Beothuks, we know little about their religious beliefs and practices.

Courtesy of the Newfoundland Museum.

The Beothuk Site at Boyd's Cove

The Boyd's Cove site, here seen across Indian Brook, was occupied by Beothuks during the late seventeenth and early eighteenth centuries. The low earth walls of houses were found on the level terrace partly obscured by trees.

Because there are so few documents that shed light on the trade that the Beothuks might have carried on, we have to turn to archaeological sites for information about this aspect—and many others—of Beothuk life. One site that has added considerably to our understanding of these people is that at Boyd's Cove which has been the subject of investigation by Memorial University archaeologists since 1982. Boyd's Cove lies on a glacial moraine (a huge deposit of soil and rocks left by a

Archaeological crew prepares to excavate a Beothuk house at Boyd's Cove. Pack ice, seen in the background, still brings polar bears to Newfoundland; bones of polar bears found at Boyd's Cove indicate that the Beothuks killed these large, powerful animals.

former glacier) deep within a maze of islands and protected reaches at the bottom of Notre Dame Bay. This site has many of the characteristics that we have come to expect of Recent Indian sites. The moraine itself consists mostly of coarse gravel about seven metres high. This means that no matter how much it rains, the water simply drains down through the subsoil leaving the surface remarkably dry.

Below the moraine a narrow beach would have made it easy to draw up fragile bark canoes. A nearby brook furnishes both fresh water and a yearly run of smelt which come there to spawn. The waters around the site still furnish soft-shelled clams, mussels, and a variety of inshore fish. Not too many years ago, harbour seals hauled out on the rocky islets just off the site and would have been a welcome addition to the diet of the site's inhabitants. Hunters living at the site could also travel about 15 kilometres to the northeast to hunt harp seals, and a few km inland to kill caribou in the water as they crossed a series of long lakes.

Fortunately, we have more than just conjecture to give us an idea of what the people of Boyd's Cove were eating. Faunal analyst Steve Cumbaa, of the National Museums of Canada Zooarchaeological Identification Centre, found that the Boyd's Cove inhabitants were dining on a remarkable variety of creatures. Although harbour seals and caribou may have been the most important mammals, the site's occupants had also feasted on beaver, black bear and polar bear. They had killed a similar range of birds including geese, cormorants, black guillemots, and a number of species of sea birds. The sea also provided these people with smelt, sculpin, sea ravens and flounder as well as soft-shelled clams and mussels.

These animal remains can also help to determine what time of the year people were living at the site. There is good evidence that Boyd's Cove was occupied from at least April to November, and it may be that it was occupied throughout the winter as well. Evidence for an early spring occupation is based, among other things, on the fact that some of the Canada geese bones showed indications of natural changes that occur just prior to egg laying—a sign that the birds may have been killed in April. The presence of polar bear remains also suggests a spring occupation since these visitors from the Arctic usually arrive on the northeast coast of Newfoundland in April and May. Similarly, the many smelt bones at Boyd's Cove are good evidence of the site's use in late April-early May, when even today the nearby brook is the scene of an impressive smelt run. It is also possible to estimate, on the basis of tooth eruption and wear, how old caribou were at the time they were killed. The evidence indicates that the Boyd's Cove hunters had killed caribou from late winter or early spring until perhaps November.

Drawing by Shanawdithit depicts Beothuk foods including dried salmon, lobster tails, a caribou skin filled with oil and seal skins with the fat still adhering.

Courtesy of the Newfoundland Museum.

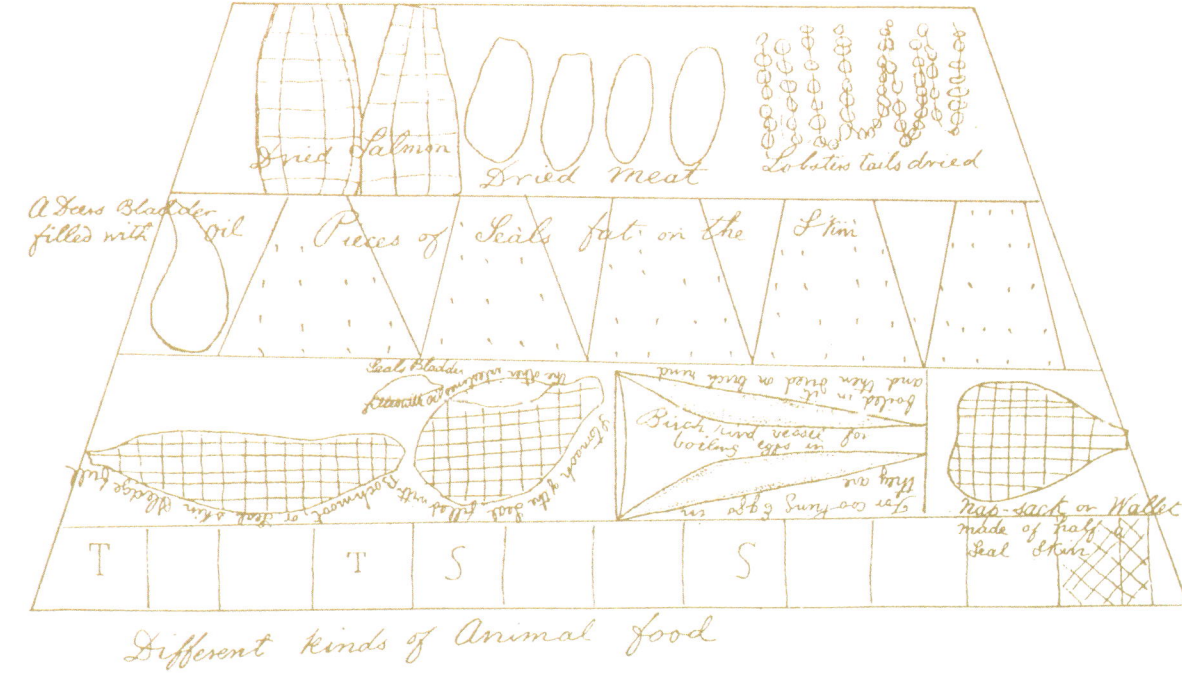

Tiny stone arrow points, although eventually to be replaced by iron examples, were still crafted by the occupants of Boyd's Cove. All of these examples were found on the living floor of a single house.

Even if the Boyd's Cove hunters and their families did not spend the winter at the site, the cold springs and autumns of the region would have been uncomfortable without adequate housing. The physical evidence indicates, in fact, that they were living in substantial, warm pit houses, eleven of which have been found at the site. Artifacts found in these houses suggest a Beothuk occupation which falls within the period about A.D. 1650 to 1720. During this time there was an English fishery to the south in Bonavista Bay and a French fishery to the west, beginning at the Baie Verte Peninsula. Boyd's Cove, in other words, was located between two European fisheries, and the debris left behind by those fisheries would have been an invaluable source of raw material for the Beothuks. In fact, that raw material was put to good use by the Boyd's Cove inhabitants. The site has produced hundreds of European nails, many of them skilfully modified into projectile points. The making of a projectile point, such as an arrow head, was begun by using a stone hammer to pound a nail against a large flat stone which would serve as an anvil. After the shaft of the nail had been flattened, the head and a small portion of the flared shaft was broken off. The blunt end of the pointed headless shaft

Nails, such as that at left in this photo, were a favoured raw material for Beothuk iron-workers. Next to the unmodified nail is one that may have been transformed into a scraper. The object in the centre is a discarded nail head. The remaining shaft has been removed by hammering, and fashioned into an arrowpoint like the two examples shown at the right.

was then shaped with an abrader stone into a thin, sharp blade, while the sharp end of the nail was left to be set into a wooden arrow or lance shaft. The object left over from this process—a head with a small piece of the shaft remaining—may have been used to scrape fat from hides.

If the abilities of the Beothuk iron workers at Boyd's Cove are impressive, their traditional stone-working skills were no less accomplished. The site's inhabitants continued to make tools like the tiny projectile points shown on page 30. They are so tiny that some have questioned whether or not they were functional, but they do not differ greatly in size from the end blades manufactured by the Dorset people some 1,000 years earlier. A small projectile point, in fact, can be more effective than a larger one because it penetrates the skin of an animal more easily. In addition to these stone projectile points, the Beothuks also made stone scrapers, bifaces, and linear flakes. The picture that we get from the Boyd's Cove tool kit, in other words, is of a people in transition between a stone and an iron technology.

These Beothuks did more than just make ordinary tools, however. Boyd's Cove has also

Bone pendant (above), as found at Boyd's Cove, shows a blunt muzzle-like 'head,' vestigial legs and a line of circles that may represent a backbone. The pendant may represent a stylized bear. Other pendants (below) were collected from Beothuk sites during the nineteenth century.

Pendants courtesy of the Newfoundland Museum.

produced a number of carved bone objects, usually referred to as pendants. It used to be thought that these pendants were made only to put in graves, but their abundance at this site suggests that they may well have been used as ornaments on the bodies and clothing of living Beothuks. The other ornaments made from local raw material were 'discoidal' shell beads—shell cut into round, quarter-sized pieces with carefully pierced holes in the centres. A number may have been strung together in a necklace—similar, perhaps, to that described by John Guy in 1612.

Unfortunately, we did not find any artifacts made from bark, leather, or fur at Boyd's Cove. This is not surprising because these items are usually preserved much better in an environment wetter than that of Boyd's Cove. Nor have we recovered any examples of European cloth, net, or rope from the site, although it is almost certain that its occupants would

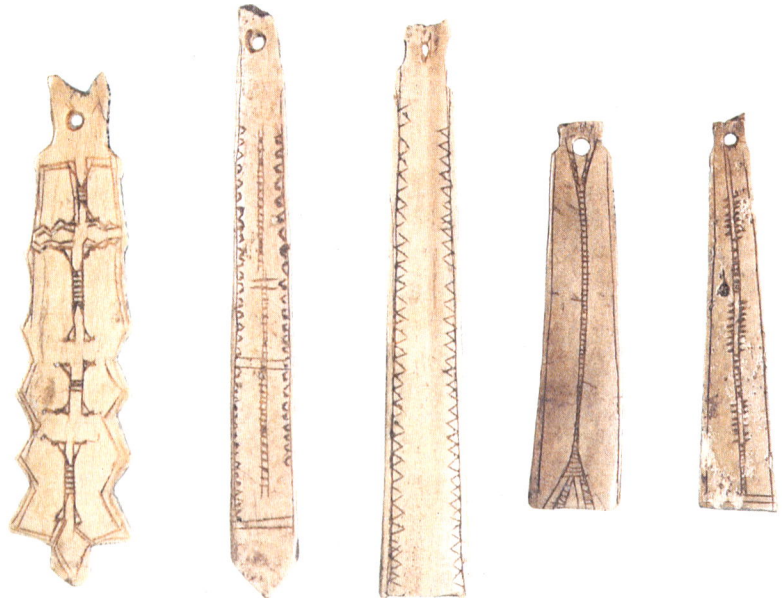

have been using these materials. In fact, the variety of European goods is unusually narrow. Elsewhere in the northeast, by contrast, an Indian site dating to the period 1650-1720 would have a much wider range of items—complete kettles, bells, rings, axes, knives, hoes, ceramic vessels, parts of firearms, and so forth. Boyd's Cove, however, has produced relatively few of these sorts of goods. Among the metal objects there are a few scraps of copper, 21 knife fragments, a portion of one axe, at least two trap parts, two dozen fish hooks and over 400 pieces of unidentified iron. The almost 1,200 nails make up the greatest number of iron objects. There are also about a dozen sherds of Normandy stoneware, a type of ceramic made in France, 25 pipe stem fragments, a few pieces of coarse earthenware, and a thimble.

Because there are so few European goods, we have found it difficult to date this site. Although we have two radiocarbon dates, one of A.D. 1810±70 on charcoal from a hearth built on top of the wall of a house after the house had been abandoned, and a date of A.D. 1680±70 from clam shells found in the entrance of one of the houses, radiocarbon dating is really too coarse a tool to be able to date historic sites with the accuracy that is needed. Historical archaeologists usually depend heavily on pottery and tobacco pipe stems to date the sites that they dig. Many European-made ceramics were in fashion for relatively short periods and thus can be quite useful in determining dates of occupation. Unfortunately, the two types of ceramics recovered from Boyd's Cove were made over a long period of time and are not very useful in determining when the site was occupied. Archaeologists have also found that, within certain limits, the diameter of English tobacco pipe stems decreases over time. In general, the wider the bore, the older the pipe. However, this method works only on English pipes and we simply do not know the origin of the Boyd's Cove pipes. Its inhabitants could just as easily have picked up the pipe stems from French as English

Small objects provide clues to Beothuk life at Boyd's Cove. Thimble with a small hole punched near the rim may have been used as a pendant or decoration. Pipe stem with fleur-de-lys within a double diamond suggests that the site was occupied during the seventeenth century.

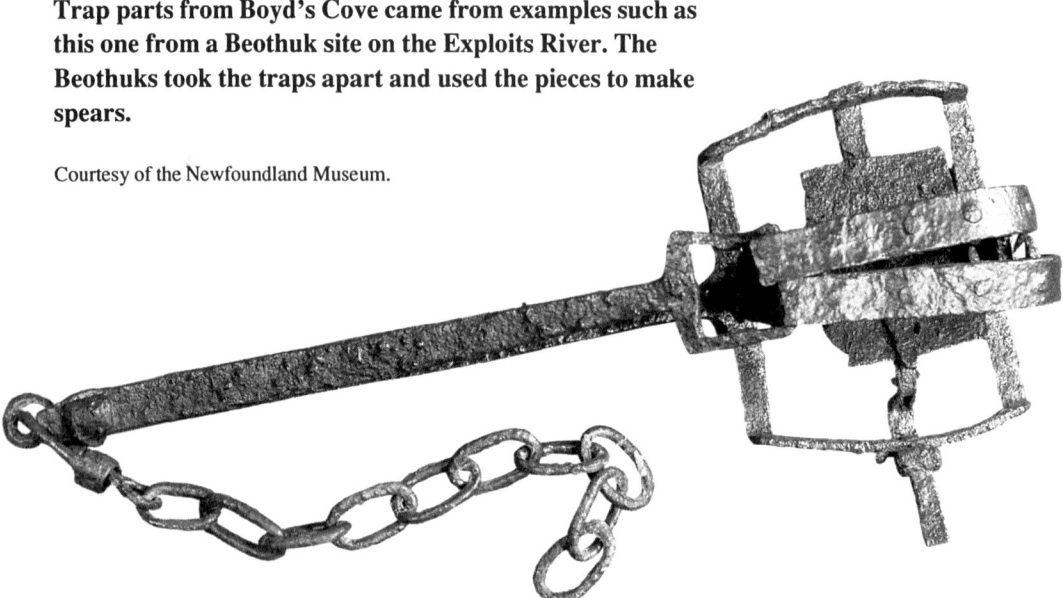

Trap parts from Boyd's Cove came from examples such as this one from a Beothuk site on the Exploits River. The Beothuks took the traps apart and used the pieces to make spears.

Courtesy of the Newfoundland Museum.

premises. Tobacco pipes can also be dated by the shape and size of the bowl, but we have not found any complete bowls at the site.

The dating of this site therefore rests on rather circumstantial evidence. Perhaps the strongest such evidence is the site's location. Beginning in 1719, an English entrepreneur named George Skeffington began a salmon fishery and fur trapping operation only six kilometres away in Dog Bay. He reported that the Beothuks had attacked his men, and we can be fairly sure that those Beothuks came from Boyd's Cove. Not long after whites moved into Dog Bay, the community of Twillingate, some 32 kilometres to the north, was founded, and we do not think that the Beothuks would have lived in highly visible pit houses along a coastline where they could have been easily seen by hostile whites. However, the site *may* have been used after the 1720s—in fact, evidence such as the hearth on the top of one house wall, and a hearth built above the living floor of another house suggests that the site was sporadically occupied after its houses were abandoned. Indeed, the archaeology of Boyd's Cove suggests a pattern that may have been followed elsewhere on the island. As spreading white settlement drove the Beothuks away from their substantial coastal pit houses, the Beothuks retreated to safer locations in the interior, but continued to visit the older sites, perhaps in smaller numbers, furtively camping in temporary wigwams out of sight of whites coasting along the shore.

With an end date for the houses' occupation of about 1720, our problem was to establish a beginning date. Here, a combination of artifactual and documentary evidence was used. A number of trap parts were recovered from the houses, and we know that European furriers began to trap in nearby Bonavista Bay not long after 1650. It is possible, of course, that the traps came from further away, in which case they may be a bit older, but it is highly unlikely that they would predate 1612. In that year one of John Guy's men began to trap furs, and as far as we know, he was the first white man to do so in Newfoundland. (The early development of fur trapping by whites is unusual in North America. Elsewhere in the seventeenth century the normal practise was for whites to trade for furs, not trap them directly. The early presence of European fur trappers is good evidence that whites had to turn to trapping furs themselves when the Beothuks became reluctant to do so.)

There are some other clues that point to an occupation in the latter part of the seventeenth century and the first two decades of the eighteenth century. The pipe stem dating formula was applied to the pipes recovered from the site, and although the sample is quite small, *if* they are English, they indicate a mean date of 1675. One of the pipe stems has a design of a fleur-de-lys inside a double diamond stamped on it. This design is most commonly found in the latter half of the seventeenth century. A thimble also found in one house—probably dropped there after the house was abandoned—is of a type manufactured at the beginning of the eighteenth century. Normandy stoneware, although made over a long period of time, tends to be more common during the seventeenth century than during other periods.

Tiny glass beads from Boyd's Cove may have been acquired by the Beothuks from Montagnais Indians from Labrador, who often visited Newfoundland during the eighteenth century.

Among the more surprising European artifacts (although not, unfortunately, datable with any precision) were some 677 blue and white glass trade beads. While we can explain the presence of all of the other European objects found at the site as the result of Beothuks scavenging from European fishing and furring premises, the presence of these beads demands another interpretation. They could have been obtained only through peaceful contact with some other group. But with whom? In 1793 one Englishman had noted that

35

Beothuk food refuse, such as this layer of clam shells, helped to buffer Newfoundland's acid soil and allowed many bone objects to survive in good condition.

'formerly' there had been a trade between his people and the Beothuks. The beads may be the result of that trade; they may also be the result of a trade between French fishermen and the Beothuks. The presence of Normandy stoneware at Boyd's Cove is a good indication that its inhabitants were *at* a French site; whether they came there to trade or to pilfer is simply not known.

Another possible explanation is that the Beothuks received these beads from another Native group. While it is conceivable that the beads may have been given to the Beothuks by the Inuit or the Micmacs, Shanawdithit, the last of the Beothuks, indicated that her people were not on good terms with either of these peoples. By contrast, she is supposed to have spoken of the 'good Indians on the other coast' by which, presumably, she meant the Montagnais. We know from French records that in the early part of the eighteenth century, a French entrepreneur based near what is now Blanc Sablon had sent a party of Montagnais over to Newfoundland to trade with the Beothuks. From the wording of his account it seems that these Montagnais were familiar with the island and its inhabitants. If this is the case it might explain the glass beads which would be one of the most portable European items that a Montagnais party could have brought with them to exchange for furs.

There is one other bit of evidence at Boyd's Cove that suggests a marginal fur trade. The soil of Newfoundland is quite acidic, and in most cases bones left behind by a site's occupants are dissolved fairly rapidly. However, because the Boyd's Cove inhabitants ate a great many clams and left their shells throughout the site, the soil is much less acidic than usual. The shells have acted much like lime to change the soil's pH, and thus bone preservation here has been excellent, and we have a fairly good idea of what animals its inhabitants were killing. Among those animals are many more fur bearers than we would have expected if the Beothuks living at Boyd's Cove were using those furs only for their own clothing. The evidence is tentative, but at the moment it is reasonable to suggest that the Boyd's Cove inhabitants may have carried on a slight fur trade with a Montagnais group from the other side of the Strait of Belle Isle.

Map of the Boyd's Cove site shows the outlines of eleven housepits visible at the site.

The beads, bones and iron from the Boyd's Cove houses provide information not only about Beothuk relations with other peoples, they can also tell us something about Beothuk society itself. Since we were able to excavate only four of the eleven houses at Boyd's Cove, the picture we have of Beothuk society at the site is incomplete. One of our greatest problems, for example, is deciding which houses were occupied at the same time. In this case, the presence or absence of trade beads may provide a clue. Since trade beads in this context would fall into the category of 'exotic

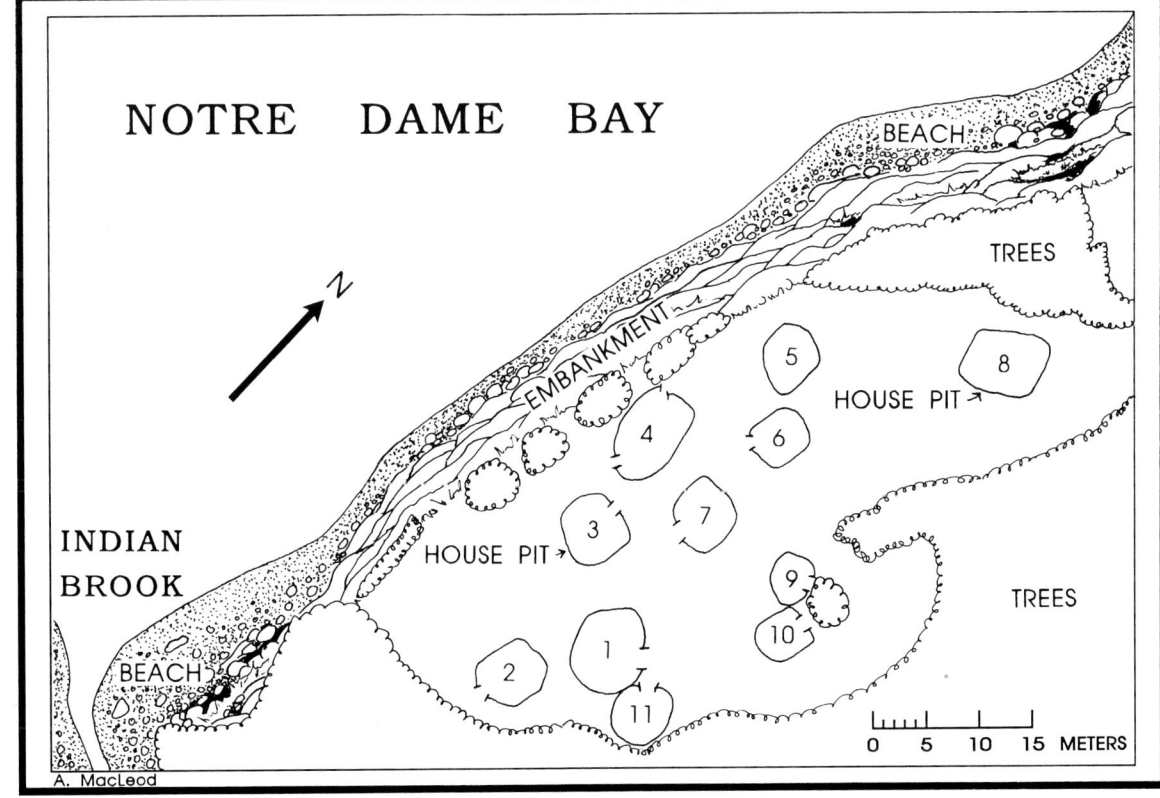

Overhead view of partially excavated House 1 shows walls and entrance. Rocks from a central hearth can be seen at the intersection of the two trenches.

goods'—relatively rare, prized objects obtained from outside the local society—we believe that such exotic goods would be shared throughout the band. If this is true, then one would expect that there would have been beads in all of the houses that were lived in at the same time. In fact, these beads are found in three of the four houses excavated.

Thus, House 11, which did not yield any trade beads, may not have been occupied when Houses 1, 3, and 4 were. House 11 is different from the other three houses in other ways as well. For example, it had a smaller proportion of stone to iron compared to the contents of the other houses. In general, Beothuk sites which contain a smaller proportion of stone to iron tend to be more recent than those from which more stone has been recovered. Thus, we think that House 11 is more recent than the others. It is also the furthest from the beach, and this too may mean that it is more recent than the others. None of the other excavated houses showed evidence (in the form of root disturbance) that they had been built within the forest. By contrast, House 11 lay partially within the bounds of the present woods, and its interior had been disturbed by the roots of trees that had fallen some time ago. Its position suggests that its builders were willing to sacrifice the convenience of living closer to the water in return for the ability to hide away from the eyes of white intruders. The depression within which House 11 sits is shallower than the others, and the angles of some of its post holes suggest that

Plan of House 1 shows pits, post holes, a sleeping hollow and a refuse deposit extending inward from the entrance.

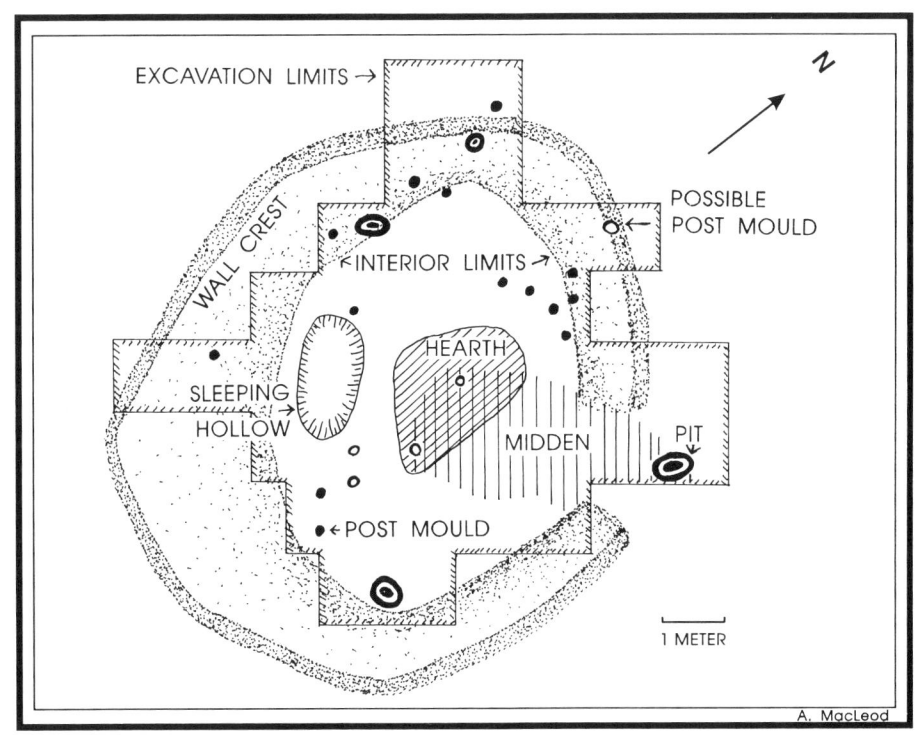

it was built as a conical wigwam—a relatively temporary structure—placed within a shallow depression, around which a ring of earth was heaped. The total amount of debris inside this house is considerably less than in the other houses, and the area of the hearth, or fire, is also smaller than the other houses. All of this suggests a house that was occupied for a shorter time than the others.

If one were to walk out of the exit/entrance to House 11, the entrance to House 1 is directly to the left—exactly where an occupant of House 11 might dispose of its garbage. In fact, in the entrance and just within the interior of House 1, was a midden consisting of a variety of animal bones and a considerable quantity of soft-shelled clam shells. Many of those shells were either whole or in large pieces, indicating that they had not been walked upon. Almost certainly then, the shells in the entrance to House 1 were not placed there by the occupants of that house, but by others—the people, we believe, who lived in House 11. Food remains, thrown by a right-handed person stepping out of House 11, would land exactly where we found it, in the entrance and just inside House 1.

This phenomenon of depositing such remains in the entrances of the houses may mean something more than just simple use of a convenient receptacle for debris. For many hunting peoples, the remains of animals, or at least some types of animals, had spiritual significance. For some peoples, it was necessary to treat the bones of certain animals with respect. Unless this were done, the animals in fu-

Excavated House 4 shows the raised central hearth, consisting of a mass of crushed bone, charcoal and fire-cracked rock.

ture would not allow themselves to be caught. For some hunting and gathering peoples as well, abandoned houses were 'special' places, marked out from the rest of the world by the fact that people had once lived in them. By depositing the remains of their food in abandoned houses, the Boyd's Cove Beothuks may have been expressing respect toward the spirits of the animals that they had killed.

We admit that this argument may sound a bit far-fetched, but this is often how archaeologists must work. Given the lack of other information about Beothuk beliefs, we have little choice but to suggest such possibilities—based on what we know about other hunting cultures—and to see if further work substantiates them. In a similar case, the shapes and sizes of the houses at Boyd's Cove have provided us with another clue, an exciting one, to Beothuk religious beliefs. Of the eleven houses at the site, all but two could be described as either roughly circular or multi-sided. The two exceptions are roughly oval in shape and larger than the others. We had already dug one small and two large multi-sided houses, and excavating one of the large oval houses would mean that we would have investigated all three of the site's house types. The large oval house nearest our earlier excavated areas was House 4, and in the summer of 1985 we decided to excavate its interior, trench its walls and dig the immediate area around it. Soon after we had begun work on House 4, we realized that this house was quite different from the others. Not only was its shape unusual, but it also proved to have two entrances, one at either end. Most surprising, instead of a roughly circular hearth in the centre, which had been the case with the other houses, House 4 had a huge, long hearth running down the central axis of the structure. The hearth consisted of a mass of tiny pieces of bone, ash, charcoal, and fire-cracked rocks. A hearth and structure of this sort are very similar to what the Naskapi-Montagnais, or Innu, of Quebec-Labrador were building until quite recently. At certain times the Innu held a special feast called a *mokoshan* to pay respect to the spirit of the caribou. The Naskapi-Montagnais believed that there was a keeper of the game, a spirit of the caribou who controlled the movements of the animal herds. Before holding a *mokoshan*, hunters collected the leg bones of caribou and during the course of the feast, the bones were ground up and boiled. The resulting grease would be skimmed off and eaten. The hearth over which this meal was taken was often either more than one fire, or a long fire which could accommodate more people than usual. Often, a *mokoshan* was held in a structure called a *shaputuan*, a large oval dwelling with two entrances.

There is some documentary evidence which might corroborate the existence of such a ritual among the Beothuks. In the winter of 1811, when Lieutenant David Buchan came upon a Beothuk camp, he found some 300 caribou leg bones on scaffolds inside the wigwams. Those bones may have been saved for a *mokoshan* feast, which in fact would have fed more than just the spiritual needs of the people. Although grinding up bones is a long tedious process, there is time for it during the winter, or during bad weather, when hunters were confined to their wigwams, and it

Large fireplace at the Daniel Rattle site, northern Labrador, may have been inside a *shaputuan*, **or ceremonial house, where a feast to honour the caribou was held.**

Courtesy of Stephen Loring.

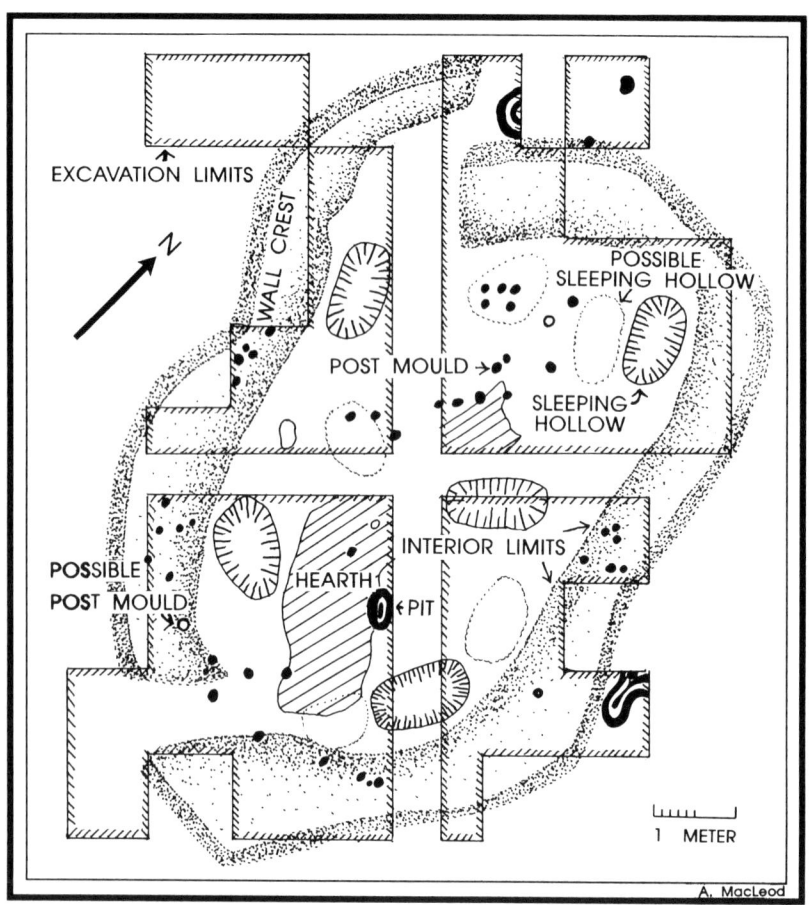

Plan of House 4 shows sleeping hollows and extent of hearth. Not all of the sleeping hollows would have been used at the same time.

yields a surprisingly nutritious food for those who consume it. There is no reason why this practise could not have both a functional and a spiritual dimension; many such types of behaviour have.

The *mokoshan* ritual may have quite ancient roots. Working at a place called Daniel Rattle on the coast of northern Labrador, the American archaeologist, Stephen Loring, discovered an oval structure about 8 metres long and 4 metres wide. Within it he found a raised hearth about 4.5 metres long and about 1 metre wide, full of ash, burnt bone, and fire-cracked rocks and tools. Although the shape and size of this structure and hearth are very close to those of House 4 at Boyd's Cove, it is perhaps six or seven hundred years older. Both structures also resemble a *shaputuan* built in the early part of this century by a central Labrador Montagnais group described by the anthropologist Frank Speck. The *shaputuan* recorded by Speck had entrances at both ends as does the Boyd's Cove house. If further work supports these connections, we may be able to substantiate an ancient element of the belief system of the Beothuks and their relatives. Although, as we have seen, Houses 4 and 11 provided tantalizing glimpses of Beothuk life, other houses at the site were almost as informative. Houses 1 and 3 are quite similar in size and shape, five to six metres in diameter, and with earthen walls about 20 centimetres high. It is clear, however, that the walls of both houses have slumped considerably, and originally would have been much higher. Both have central hearths which were made by excavating a slight depression and building a fire in it. These two houses (and House 1) contained surprisingly little debris associated with their hearths. Large amounts of small, fire-cracked rocks were found outside of these houses, however, and we believe that these rock concentrations are the result of periodic cleaning out of the hearth areas when the rocks became too small to hold the heat adequately. House 1, for example, has what appears to be a very large hearth, but we are fairly sure that this does not mean that it contained a huge fire. Rather, we believe that the actual position of the fire changed somewhat over time. In all cases, however, where a fire had been burning for a long period of time, the subsoil was burnt red in colour and this proved to be an good indicator of where the actual fire had been.

Archaeologist at left carefully excavates in House 3; person in centre maps an excavated one-metre square, while the archaeologist in the background records information in field notes.

The interiors of all of the houses (except House 11) contained sleeping hollows, similar to those described by eighteenth century European observers. Those at Boyd's Cove are shallow depressions, oval in shape and just over a metre in length. One in House 4 seems to have been excavated, but this may only be because the hearth had spread over the area and it was necessary to clear away the debris. Sleeping hollows in other houses may have come about simply as the result of people continually sleeping in a particular spot. Over time, the weight of the individual would so pack down the soil that years later it would be discoverable by the archaeologist. If it were possible to locate all of the sleeping hollows, it would be a relatively easy job to calculate the number of individuals each of these houses contained. Unfortunately, things are seldom that simple. In House 11, for example, we were unable to locate any sleep-

Circles of string outline sleeping hollows in the floor of excavated House 3.

Discovering the number of occupants of each house would be a great help to our understanding of Beothuk society at Boyd's Cove, but for a number of reasons, that has proven to be a difficult, if not impossible, task. There is, for example, clear evidence that the number of occupants in some of the houses varied over time. Post holes were found in some sleeping hollows, but whether the posts were placed there before or after the depressions were used as sleeping hollows is impossible to determine. What is clear, however, is that these areas were sometimes needed as sleeping places, and others times not. The inescapable conclusion is that the number of occupants per house varied.

Potentially, House 11 might have been able to hold 10 or 11 individuals; House 1, 12 or 13 people; House 3, about the same, and House 4, perhaps 15. These are maximum figures, based on the number of people who could have curled up around a fire in areas the

ing hollows, although we were able to find areas between the hearth and the walls which were level and relatively free of small rocks, and other debris. These we referred to as 'sleeping areas.' In House 1, only one sleeping hollow could be seen; others almost certainly were obscured by the debris later thrown into the house. While some of the sleeping hollows in Houses 3 and 4 were quite clear, others were not, and in the plans of these houses were marked with question marks. These questionable sleeping hollows, tended to be quite free of artifacts and stone and iron debris, however, and it seems reasonable to conclude that they were sleeping areas.

size of known sleeping hollows. Thus, the number of sleeping hollows may not represent the number of individuals living in a house at any given time. We do, however, have some documentary evidence about the actual capacity of Beothuk houses. Shanawdithit, the last known Beothuk, said that in 1811 the main camp that Buchan visited had three wigwams, two of which had 15 people each, while the third held 12. In another settlement, 13 individuals were living in two wigwams, while at a third camp, two wigwams housed 9 and 8 people. It should be noted, however, that these figures come from a time when the Beothuks may have been crowded together as refugees in a limited number of houses—perhaps because of the smallness, and possibly even the poor health, of the band. A small number of survivors, weakened by disease and malnutrition, might not have been able to build and maintain the substantial structures that had been characteristic of their culture at an earlier date.

Winter wigwam reconstructed at Indian Point, Red Indian Lake, with earthen wall banked around vertical posts, resembles Houses 1 and 3 at Boyd's Cove.

Not only are we unable to calculate the exact number of inhabitants per house, we also do not yet know the number of occupants living at Boyd's Cove at any one time. Based on present evidence, we think that there might be two groupings of five houses, and one lone house (House 11). If the two large, oval houses are *shaputuans*, it is likely that they were used as such by the inhabitants of a cluster of houses. It seems unlikely that there would have been two *shaputuans* in use at the same time. Two clusters of five houses (occupied at different times), each with its own *shaputuan*, might have had anywhere from 6 to 12 inhabitants per house. This would result in a community of from 30 to 60 people during the period of

Exploits River, in central Newfoundland, supported a remnant Beothuk population until the early nineteenth century.

the site's maximum use. At a somewhat later date, House 11 might have been built by a single family using Boyd's Cove after the occupation of the rest of the site. Nonetheless, unless all of the site is excavated, it will not be possible to have any real confidence about these population estimates—and even then we probably could never say for certain which houses were occupied at the same time.

These uncertainties aside, the picture that emerges at Boyd's Cove, in the words of the site's faunal analyst, Stephen Cumbaa, is 'a glimpse of a people at ease in their environment and obviously exercising a fair degree of control over use of its resources. The contrasting picture we have a century later of a beleaguered and dwindling population eking out a living on the run from a dominant culture is all the sadder for the comparison.' In order to understand how the Beothuks came to this end, it is necessary to examine their history.

The Extinction of the Beothuks

We may never know when the Beothuks first met Europeans, but it is quite possible that the first Europeans to be encountered by the Beothuks, or their ancestors, were the Norse who visited Labrador and Newfoundland in the eleventh century and perhaps later. The Norse in Scandinavia and Iceland wrote versions of earlier epic oral tales, called sagas, and these accounts mention contact between the Norse and Native people, although it is not clear if these contacts occurred in Newfoundland. However, Newfoundland boasts the only undisputed Norse site in North America, that of L'Anse aux

Copy of earlier portrait of Mary March may have been influenced by artist William Gosse's acquaintance with Shanawdithit, the last known Beothuk.

Courtesy of the Mary March Regional Museum.

Norse settlers, who lived briefly in buildings such as these reconstructed sod houses at L'Anse aux Meadows, Newfoundland, may have contacted ancestors of the Beothuks. Except for accounts in the *Sagas,* however, no evidence for these contacts has been found.

Meadows, which dates to about 1000 years ago. This now well-known site at the top of Newfoundland's Great Northern Peninsula appears to have been a boat repair station occupied for a relatively short period by a Norse expedition which earlier had been further south in the Gulf of St. Lawrence. There is no archaeological evidence of contact between the Norse and the Little Passage people at L'Anse aux Meadows, but a stone projectile point of a style similar to those used by Indian peoples of southern Labrador and Newfoundland, at about the time of the site's occupation, has been found on a beach in Greenland below a Norse graveyard which was eroding out into the beach. It is possible, as the Arctic archaeologist, Robert McGhee, has suggested, that this was an Indian arrowhead brought to Greenland by a Norseman who had actually encountered Indians in southern Labrador or Newfoundland.

We may not know the extent, if any, of contact between the Norse and the ancestors of the Beothuks (or their close cousins), but we can be reasonably sure that any such contact did not materially affect Indian culture. Nothing in the archaeological record hints at any major disruption or change in Indian culture at the time when the Norse could have been expected to have met them. By contrast, the arrival of the next Europeans, fishermen and explorers from western Europe, would have a significant impact on the life of the Beothuks.

A few historians have argued that Bristol mariners had found Newfoundland a decade before Columbus's discovery of the New World in 1492, but we have no real proof that they actually did. Until we have hard evidence to the contrary, it appears that the first European to visit the Gulf of St. Lawrence was John Cabot in 1497. Cabot saw Native people from his ship and found the remains of a fire and a few artifacts on land, but we cannot be completely sure that Cabot actually visited Newfoundland or that he saw Beothuks. Because of a lack of geographic and ethnographic knowledge, the accounts from other early sixteenth century explorers are quite vague as to where they were and what Native peoples they had observed. Mention of terms such as the 'New Found Land,' 'Terra Nova,' and the like in the documents of the first decades of the sixteenth century is not conclusive evidence that the explorers in question actually came to Newfoundland. At the time, the word 'Newfoundland' and similar terms did not necessarily refer to a specific island, but instead to a general area. One of the first unambiguous references to Beothuks appears to be that of Jacques Cartier in 1534. Cartier, following a dream which would last for centuries, had been sent by the King of France to find a way by sea to the riches of the Orient. He put in at Bonavista Bay, in Newfoundland, and visited the Funk Islands, where hundreds of thousands of sea birds nested. As the Nova Scotia ethnohistorian, Ruth Whitehead, has noted, Cartier reported that the Beothuk word for the great auk (once found in enormous numbers on Funk Island) was *apponath*. Cartier had been to Newfoundland before, and his use of a Native word for a local bird species suggests that the fishermen from western Europe who had been attracted to the Gulf soon after Cabot's trip had already encountered the region's Native people and that at least some of those meetings were peaceful.

Jacques Cartier's use, in 1534, of the Beothuk word *apponath* for the great auk suggests early contacts between Beothuks and European fishermen.

Courtesy of the Newfoundland Museum.

Although not all fishing premises were as elaborate as this 1705 example, most would have furnished an ample supply of nails and other raw materials which the Beothuks fashioned into tools and weapons.

Courtesy of Shane O'Dea.

By the late 1520s at least, men from England, Spain, Portugal, and France were in Newfoundland carrying on what has been called a 'dry fishery'—as opposed to a 'wet fishery.' Fishing from large ships far from shore and salting the fish in the holds was referred to as a wet fishery, since the fish were packed away in a 'wet' condition. Ships following a wet fishery seldom had need to come ashore except occasionally for fresh water and perhaps wood. In a dry fishery, however, the cod were caught by men fishing in small boats close to shore and the fish were dried on 'flakes' on shore and only lightly salted. This meant that these fishermen came to Newfoundland in the spring and built cabins, wharves, stages, and flakes on land. After the season ended, they left for their homes in Europe, and left behind some of the nails, fish hooks, and the like that the Beothuks treasured. We may have very early evidence of this practise at a site in the modern community of Ferryland. Here, crews from Memorial University have unearthed stone tools associated with an Indian hearth. The Indian occupation was at the same level as the earliest European occupation—quite probably in the sixteenth century—and it is possible that this is evidence of an early Beothuk group visiting an abandoned fishing premises to scavenge for European metal. Shipwrecks also were a source of European goods as attested by the account of the *Grace*, whose crew in 1594 saw in St. George's Bay, on the west coast of the island, the wrecks of two Basque ships and a Beothuk camp nearby—almost certainly to take advantage of the materials that a ship would have provided.

The countrymen of the unfortunate Basques who crewed those two ships had for some time been whaling in the Strait of Belle Isle at places such as Red Bay. Here, a team of archaeologists under the direction of Memorial University's James Tuck has thoroughly investigated a large Basque whaling station, occupied from about 1540 to about 1600, which may also have been visited by the Beothuks or their close relatives. Memorial researchers have found dozens of hearths among the remains of Basque structures. The tools found with these hearths are similar to those made by the Little Passage people on the island, and the Red Bay Natives may be simply Beothuks who lived on the Labrador side of the Strait of Belle Isle. Tuck has not found evidence of trade between these Natives and the Basque whalers at Red Bay; instead, the hearths appear to belong to Indians who were picking up European goods on site at the end of the whaling season when the Basques had gone back to Spain.

Reconstructed frame of a sixteenth century whaling station at Red Bay, Labrador was surrounded by Indian hearths. Some contained European, as well as Native goods, suggesting that Natives camped there to obtain iron and other European materials.

There is a possibility, however, that there were peaceful relations between the Basques and the Indians who frequented the region. In an account written in 1622, but referring to earlier events, Richard Whitbourne, a promoter of English settlement in the island, noted that in the 'north and west part of the country…the French and Biscaines (who resort thither yearly for the whale-fishing and also for the cod-fish) report them to be an ingenious and tractable people (being well-used); they are ready to assist them with great labour and patience in killing, cutting, and boiling of whales; and making the

Hearth and stone flakes, found beneath this seventeenth century wall at Ferryland, on Newfoundland's eastern Avalon Peninsula, may be evidence of Beothuks who camped there to scavenge European items when the fishermen had returned to Europe during the winter months.

traine oyle, without expectation of other reward than a little bread or some such small hire.'

The documentary evidence suggests a few more examples of early peaceful contacts between the Beothuks and the new white arrivals, but until we come to the seventeenth century, these accounts are very brief and not always clear. By the early seventeenth century, however, the Beothuks begin to emerge from the vague reports of the explorers and mariners of the previous century. Beginning in 1610, a number of English entrepreneurs began schemes to plant colonies in Newfoundland. Unlike the fishermen who went back to England every fall with their catch, these people attempted to stay the entire year, and some of them, at least, kept detailed records of their stay on the island. One of them, a would-be colonizer named John Guy, came across Beothuk wigwams and then a group of Beothuks themselves at the bottom of Trinity Bay in October of 1612.

Recent archaeological research directed by William Gilbert appears to confirm an earlier supposition that one of the sites where Guy's men found Beothuk houses was on the shores of Dildo Pond in the modern community of Blaketown. There the Englishmen found a copper kettle, seal skins, fur clothing, a sail and a fishing reel—clear evidence of the previous contact with other Europeans. Unfortunately, we cannot be sure how the Beothuks acquired those European goods. Later, as we shall see, the

Beothuks appeared to have obtained most of their European metal by pilfering from fishing premises that were abandoned when English fishermen went back to their West Country homes in the fall of the year. The materials that were found in these Dildo Pond houses, however, suggest that these Beothuks had been participating in a fur trade with Europeans. The fact that an entire kettle was numbered amongst the house's possessions suggests that it was a trade item since it is unlikely that migratory fishermen would have left behind a whole kettle. One of the Beothuk structures was covered with a sail, another item also unlikely to have been casually discarded. Guy's people also found 'a little peece of fleshe' which they later discovered to be 'a beaver cod'—probably the perineal gland from which was made castoreum, a valuable substance used in the making of perfume. These glands were trade items elsewhere in North America, and the Dildo Pond Beothuks may have been drying the beaver perineal glands to exchange for European goods.

After travelling up Bull Arm in the bottom of the western side of Trinity Bay, Guy at last met a party of Beothuks, eight in number, in two canoes. This meeting may have occurred near the archaeological site at Frenchman's Island, investigated by Memorial archaeologists under the direction of Clifford Evans in the early 1980s. The Beothuks Guy encountered had clearly dealt with Europeans before. One of the Indians walked toward the white men shaking a wolf skin—in somewhat the same way as a European would proceed under a white flag. Once peaceful contact was made, the Indians danced and leapt about, clear-

Russell's Point site, on Dildo Pond in eastern Newfoundland, may have been the place where pioneer settler John Guy encountered Beothuks in 1612.

Frenchman's Island, Trinity Bay, may have been the scene of an early encounter between John Guy's colonists and the Beothuks.

Courtesy of Clifford Evans.

ly happy with the proceedings. They presented Guy's men with a chain of shells, a knife, a feather, and a headless arrow (a symbol of peace?). The Englishmen responded by presenting the Beothuks with a knife, a piece of brass and food and drink. In a touching episode, the humanity of which resonates down the centuries to us, one of the Indians sent his companions into gales of laughter by blowing into a liquor bottle. After a further exchange of presents, the two groups parted at nightfall. It is clear that the Beothuks had come to this meeting intending to trade seriously rather than just exchange presents, for the Englishmen later found that the Indians had erected a small tent, put up a dozen poles and hung furs and chains of shells on them. Guy's men seem to have thought that the Indians had done this to dry the furs, and only later realized that the Beothuks had expected the Europeans to leave goods behind in return for the furs.

Since the Beothuks had intended for the actual exchange to have taken place while they were away, it is possible that they had fallen into a pattern of trade called 'silent barter.' When two groups are suspicious of each other, they have sometimes exchanged goods by leaving displays of items and having the other party deposit the desired goods without face-to-face contact. In 1793, long after Guy's meeting with Beothuks, an English explorer and entrepreneur named George Cartwright stated that 'formerly a very beneficial barter was carried on between our people… leaving goods at a certain place, and the Indians taking what

Somewhat fanciful engraving by German Theodore de Bry dates from 1627-28 and depicts an encounter between John Guy and the Beothuks.

Courtesy of Shane O'Dea.

they wanted and leaving furs in return.' It is possible that this is how the Beothuks might have begun trade with Europeans that they did not know; once they were satisfied as to the Europeans' intentions, a more normal sort of trade might have taken place.

Although Guy's meeting with the Beothuks was brief and he did not encounter them again, he provided us with the first clear picture of their appearance and equipment. He was so taken by their canoes, in fact, that he stole one left behind by its owners. Although Guy had behaved relatively well compared to other Europeans of his day, a great deal of effort had gone into the making of that canoe, and Guy's theft of it was typical of the cavalier way Europeans of the period treated Indians.

That attitude toward Natives may have been part of the reason why the Beothuks would later avoid contact with Europeans. Since most of the fishermen who came to Newfoundland were not literate, we will never know about all of the incidents in which Europeans assaulted Indians and stole their goods. Such incidents undoubtedly occurred, however, and may have been the reason why, after John Guy's meeting with the Beothuks in 1612, they almost disappear from the historical record until the middle of the eighteenth century. In 1622, the mariner and promoter of European settlement, Richard Whitbourne, reported that there were no Beothuks living on the Avalon peninsula. In fact he said that 'there is not the least signe or appearance, that euer there was any habitation of the Sauages, or that they euer came into those parts, to the Southward of Trinity

Bay.' Whitbourne may have been exaggerating the lack of an Indian presence in order to encourage white settlement, but it is clear that as permanent settlement spread north and west, the Beothuks retreated from the growing white communities.

But the question of why the Beothuks withdrew from white contact with such determination remains. Everywhere else in seventeenth century North America, contacts between Europeans and Native people resulted in bloodshed, attacks on Native beliefs, alcoholism, disease, and a host of other traumas. And yet the Native people thus affected did not avoid Europeans; quite the contrary, they sought them out to trade for the guns, kettles, knives, blankets and axes that made their lives a great deal easier. As we have seen, Beothuk interaction with whites was not like this at all. While there appears to have been a sporadic trade which on some occasions may have taken the form of silent barter, nothing like the full-scale trade that developed on the mainland took place in Newfoundland. What was different about the island?

The major reason for the difference in Indian-white relations in Newfoundland, compared to the rest of North America, appears to lie in the nature of the early Newfoundland economy. As we have seen, for more than two hundred years most of the fishermen who came to Newfoundland exploited the island's resources on a seasonal basis and in doing so left behind the raw materials for Beothuk tools. As a result, the Beothuks did not *need* to trade furs for European metal objects, instead they could pilfer them from abandoned fishing premises. There were real advantages to obtaining European goods through scavenging rather than trade. Combing seasonally abandoned fishing stations meant that the Beothuks would not have to spend valuable time hunting fur-bearing animals instead of hunting larger ones for food. It also meant that they did not have to suffer the violence and disease that accompanied fur trading transactions elsewhere in North America. There were, however, dangers to this strategy in the long run. Most importantly, European fishermen came to regard the Beothuks as habitual thieves. At a time when governments in Europe punished thievery with extreme savagery, whites in Newfoundland were not inclined to look with tolerance on what they regarded as the theft of the goods they needed to survive. Thus, even though the pattern of pilfering from fishing premises proved successful in the short run, as European settlement on the island increased, so also did conflict with the Beothuks. The absence of a long history of face-to-face trade meant that the two peoples had not evolved ways of peacefully settling disputes, and as a result when whites armed with guns met Beothuks, the usual outcome was that the Beothuks fled. To avoid these hostile encounters, the

William Richmond gave me the following account.

"Thomas Taylor, my Brother Richard, James Lilly, William Hooper, Dumb Jack, Nicholas Stone, James Green & myself set out on a Tuesday Morning with our Guns, Provisions &c. fully resolved to kill every Indian we might see both big & small; in order to be revenged on them for killing Thomas Rowsell, & pilfering from us as they do: but (bless God) our consciences when we came to the Point would not suffer us to do it. We travelled up the main Brook until Saturday, & walked about 20 Miles each day: for it was as good walking as ever I knew it on the Ice. We walked from Sunrise to Sunset, stopping only a few Minutes now & then, to eat a mouthfull of Bread & take a Draught at the Water falls, which are always open. When we come to one of these Falls, we take the Path made by the Indians to go round it. The day before we came up with the Indians, we saw their traces in the Snow; & then we were unanimous in our determination to kill all we should come across. — On Saturday we saw their footsteps recently imprinted

Selection from a 1792 manuscript produced by Lt. George C. Pulling illustrates Europeans' perception of the Beothuks in the late eighteenth century. Pulling went to the northeast coast of Newfoundland to report on Beothuk-European relations and recorded a number of attacks on the Beothuks.

Courtesy of the Public Archives of Newfoundland and Labrador.

This portion of the manuscript refers to a William Richmond, one of a number of fishermen/furriers who carried out a raid against a group of Beothuks in Exploits Bay. In their attack on a Beothuk camp, the settlers killed a Beothuk man, wounded a boy and captured a young girl.

Ancestors of these early twentieth century Micmacs may have come to Newfoundland from Cape Breton as long ago as the sixteenth century.

Courtesy of the Public Archives of Newfoundland and Labrador.

Beothuks appear to have moved their camps and hunting and fishing grounds away from areas of permanent white settlement.

A strategy of withdrawal could not be successful in the long run. The resources of the island are not spread along the coasts and lands of the interior evenly. There are prime locations where salmon, caplin, smelt, harbour seals, shellfish, and the like are available, but once those locations were preempted by white settlers, the total amount of food available for the Beothuks was that much more reduced.

Thus far we have concentrated on the threat to Beothuk culture posed by English settlement. The English, however, were but one of the competitors for the island's resources. According to the best understanding we have of today's archaeological evidence, before A.D. 1500 the Beothuks had the island of Newfoundland to themselves. The stone tools of prehistoric

Beothuks have been found all around the island with the possible exception of the eastern Avalon peninsula. After the discovery of the New World by Europeans, however, the Beothuks would increasingly have to deal with other, intrusive groups settling on the island. The English were first, but the French established a permanent settlement at Placentia by 1662, depriving the Beothuks of free access to the grey and harbour seals of the great Bay of Placentia. (Reports of the Governors of Placentia indicate that by the end of the seventeenth century they had very little knowledge of the Beothuks other than what they had been told by the Micmacs.)

The arrival of the Micmacs would also have caused further stress to the Beothuks. Formerly it was widely believed that the French brought the Micmacs to Newfoundland as mercenaries and even paid the Micmacs a bounty for the taking of Beothuk heads. There is no direct evidence that this ever happened. In fact, it is quite clear that the Micmacs began coming to Newfoundland for their own reasons—essentially to hunt and trap in the interior—and no evidence from French sources has been unearthed which would support the charge that bounties were paid for Beothuk heads.

Just when the Micmacs began coming to Newfoundland is a matter of some dispute. There is no doubt that Micmacs from Cape Breton could have come to Newfoundland in prehistoric times; the presence of aboriginal tools on the Magdalen Islands, a comparable distance from the mainland of

Small sailing vessels, like these seventeenth century shallops were used by the Micmacs to travel throughout the Gulf of St. Lawrence and beyond.

From D.W. Prowse, *History of Newfoundland.*

Nova Scotia, indicates that the Micmacs could have made the eighty mile trip across the Cabot Strait in birchbark canoes. However, as yet there is no archaeological evidence to confirm this. Since prehistoric Beothuk tools have been recovered from just those areas in Newfoundland where the Micmacs settled, the implication is that in prehistoric times those areas were occupied by the ancestors of the Beothuks, not the Micmacs. There is no doubt, however, that Micmacs were coming to Newfoundland as early as 1601, and almost certainly earlier. Their arrival may be linked to over-hunting of furbearers and game in Cape Breton, and also to the availability to the Micmacs of shallops—small European sailing vessels which the Micmacs very early learned to use. Such craft would have made the hazardous trip across the Cabot Strait a much safer journey. Eventually, the Micmacs appear to have established an extension of their hunting territory ranging from Bay St. George in the west, across the southern part of the island to Placentia Bay. We have evidence from Shanawdithit, the last known member of the Beothuks, that her people feared the Micmacs, and it seems clear that a Micmac presence in southern Newfoundland would have denied the Beothuks access to the harbour and grey seals of the south coast as well as the large interior caribou herds that even today winter on the windswept barrens inland from the coast.

The Micmacs were not the only Native people to impact on the Beothuks in the historic period. As early as the sixteenth century the Inuit of Labrador had begun to visit, and perhaps stay, in the Strait of Belle Isle. According to Shanawdithit, the Beothuks were not on good terms with the Inuit, and their use of the Strait of Belle Isle might also have prevented the Beothuks from exploiting the seals and sea birds of what one authority has aptly called the 'resource funnel' of the Gulf of St. Lawrence. Thus,

Seal vertebrae strung on a rib were part of a game played by Inuit at Red Bay, Labrador during the sixteenth century. Inuit probably visited seasonally abandoned whaling stations to obtain European goods. The object of the typical Inuit game was to toss the vertebrae in the air and catch them on the rib.

by the end of the seventeenth century, the Beothuk domain had shrunk considerably. Now they were effectively confined to Notre Dame Bay, although, of course, hunting and scavenging trips to Bonavista Bay would still be possible, as would expeditions to interior locations such as Red Indian Lake, to take caribou and beaver. This shrinking range implies a corresponding shrinkage in the total Beothuk population, although we cannot be sure of the actual numbers. In this regard, it is almost certainly incorrect to think of a single Beothuk group inhabiting just the island of Newfoundland over a long period of time. A more likely picture would have been a number of bands scattered around the coast and on the other side of the Strait of Belle Isle—the members of which traded meat, furs, raw materials, and marriage partners with each other. After the arrival of the English, French, and others, these bands would have lost members and eventually died out, or their survivors would have consolidated with other bands. Eventually, the Beothuks may have consisted of a single large group made up of the remnants of former bands. For this final group, the loss of potential marriage partners might have been one of their most serious dilemmas. Once the numbers of an ethnic group sink below a certain number, the difficulties of maintaining the group can become overwhelming and the end result is extinction.

We begin to see the first documentary evidence of that process of extinction in the records of the middle of the eighteenth century. By that time the face of Newfoundland had begun to change

Spoon, saw blade and scissors from a Beothuk site on the Exploits River were almost certainly stolen from a Newfoundland settler's home. They help explain the hostility between Beothuks and settlers.

Hugh Palliser, naval governor of Newfoundland from 1764 to 1768, was the first government official to attempt to end the hostilities between Europeans and Beothuks.

Courtesy of the Public Archives of Newfoundland and Labrador.

forever. Most importantly, the resident European population—those who lived all year round on the island—had increased dramatically since the beginning of the seventeenth century. Many of the new residents now lived in Bonavista Bay, on Fogo Island, and in Twillingate—they were, in other words, encroaching on the last coastal refuge of the Beothuks. Those whites who stayed the winter went inland to cut wood, hunt caribou, and to trap furs, and to the outer headlands and islands to kill seals. Increasingly they were trespassing upon what had once been Beothuk land. In summer the resident Europeans were now fishing not only for cod but for salmon as well. When whites netted the mouths of salmon streams along the northeast coast, they were taking food away from the men, women, and children who still tried to follow the old pattern of moving from one food supply to another when each became available in turn.

What must have been most frightening to those last Beothuk bands, however, was simply that, increasingly, they encountered whites everywhere—in the interior where the caribou crossed the lakes and rivers, on the ponds where beavers built their lodges, along the salmon streams, and on the headlands and offshore islands where seals hauled up and sea birds nested. Both groups now assumed the worst when they sighted each other, and all too frequently, there were casualties on both sides. Since the Europeans had firearms and the Beothuks did not, however, the Beothuks suffered much more in these encounters.

But by the middle of the eighteenth century, in contrast to the previous century, the killing of Natives did not go unnoticed. Two things were different. First, the island now had the beginnings of a government in the form of a naval governor. Second, the attitudes of at least some Europeans had changed. There was still a great deal of inhumanity, to be sure, but throughout the North Atlantic world there was a new concern for the casualties of western society. At about this time we see the emergence of anti-slavery societies and a growing realization on the part of people such as Quakers, Moravians, and a few others, that great wrongs had been done to the Native people of the New World.

One of those people was Hugh Palliser, the naval governor of Newfoundland from 1764 to 1768. He was instrumental in bringing the Moravians to Labrador—at least in part to prevent clashes between Europeans and the Inuit. Shocked at what he found in Newfoundland, he wrote to the home government in 1766 reporting that the "barbarous system of killing prevails amongst our People towards the native Indians…whom our People always kill, when they can meet them." Whites *were* killing Beothuks, it is true, but his statement was an exaggeration which was partly the result of his prejudice against fishermen who had chosen to settle in Newfoundland. In Palliser's eyes, the ideal Newfoundland would have been a base for a migratory fishery and a "nursery for British seamen." In any case, it is unlikely that he understood the complex interplay of factors which had operated to bring Indian-white relations to this state in the middle of the eighteenth century. Palliser did,

George Cartwright (1739-1819), former British army officer, and his brother were sent by Palliser to make contact with the Beothuks in 1768.

From George Cartwright, *A Journal of Transactions and Events…on the Coast of Labrador.*

One of the Beothuks' last winter villages was located at Indian Point on Red Indian Lake near the source of the Expolits River.

however, understand what had to be done; contact had to be made with the Beothuks, and they had to be reassured that the government, at least, would try to protect them. To do this he sent two military men, the brothers John and George Cartwright, on an expedition up the Exploits River to make contact with the Beothuks. Although the Cartwrights found deserted camps all along the river, they failed to meet a single Indian. Based on what they had seen, they believed that there were between 400 and 500 Beothuks still living in the region. In fact, this estimate was only an informed guess; other authorities, such as the ethnohistorian, Ingeborg Marshall, have suggested a lower figure.

We will probably never know what the actual Beothuk population was in 1768, the year of the Cartwrights' unsuccessful expedition, but we can be sure that it was declining, and that the now official government policy of trying to make contact with the Beothuks was not working. Following Palliser, a succession of governors issued proclamations forbidding the settlers to persecute the Indians and offering rewards to anyone bringing a Native captive into a white settlement for the purpose of establishing friendly relations between the two peoples.

Although the official policy of attempting to secure Beothuk individuals failed, there were several cases of kidnapped Beothuks living among the whites. Possibly the reverse was also true. Elsewhere in North America, Native peoples who were still independent of white domination occasionally incorporated white captives into their society. This, too, may have occurred in Newfoundland; in the winter of 1811, during the course of the only contact made between a representative of the Newfoundland government and the Beothuks, Lt. David Buchan reported that one of the women in the Beothuk camp was 'a female bearing all the appearance of an European, with light sandy hair, and features strongly similar to the French…'

That sandy-haired woman might have been a European captive—or the descendant of one—and we can be reasonably sure that she was obtained through an act of violence, as was the case with Beothuk captives obtained by the white settlers. Unfortunately, for the rest of the century and into the next, violence would be the dominant theme in Beothuk-settler encounters. This was vividly revealed in a report produced by Naval Lieutenant George C. Pulling who in 1792 collected a number of testimonies from the northeast coast. The report is a sad litany of whites stealing from Beothuk wigwams and murdering their inhabitants, punctuated by sporadic references to Beothuks stealing from fishermen and furriers and occasionally loosing arrows at them. As Pulling put it: 'In short the people who reside at this part of Newfoundland seem to think it no crime to take away the life or the property of those unenlightened wretches for they look on them as a race of men who take every opportunity to injure them and think it right and doing themselves justice to retaliate.' Pulling's assessment was unfortunately correct. European settlers feared the Beothuks and

Reproduction of a painting made for Governor Holloway in 1808. The original was to be shown to the Beothuks to encourage friendly relations.

Courtesy of the Newfoundland Museum.

resented what appeared to be their gratuitous thievery; the Beothuks, on the other hand, were simply acquiring the European goods as they had for over a hundred years. The difference now was that the white intruders had preempted the coasts and rivers that for hundreds of years had furnished the Beothuks with food. The Beothuks faced a further danger in that by the end of the eighteenth century, many white settlers on the northeast coast were intimately familiar with waters and woods of the island. No longer were the Beothuks pilfering from migratory English fishermen, now they had to contend with whites who were almost as at home in the Newfoundland environment as they were. Such people made dangerous enemies.

That enmity between the settlers and the Beothuks continued into the nineteenth century, despite the proclamations from St. John's calling for peaceful relations and a reward for the capture of a Beothuk who could then be turned into an emissary to bring to the Beothuks word that the government wanted to break the chain of pilferage and murder. There was a possibility that peaceful contact could have been made in 1803 when William Cull, a fisherman and furrier captured a Beothuk woman and brought her to St. John's for the governor's promised reward. The unnamed woman spent some time in St. John's where she was given presents, and Cull was told to return her to her people in the hopes of convincing them of the government's good will. Cull, however, kept the woman at his home on Fogo Island for about a year before finally depositing her on the banks of the Exploits River, where, presumably, her people would come to take her back. As Frederick Rowe, the noted Newfoundland historian and descendant of northeast coast settlers, concluded, a 'golden opportunity to put European-Beothuk relations on a peaceful footing had been lost.'

Sketch by Shanawdithit depicts the Buchan expedition to Red Indian Lake in 1811. It reveals information not in Buchan's account, such as the fact that the Beothuks placed the head of one of Buchan's marines on a pole and danced around it.

Courtesy of the Newfoundland Museum.

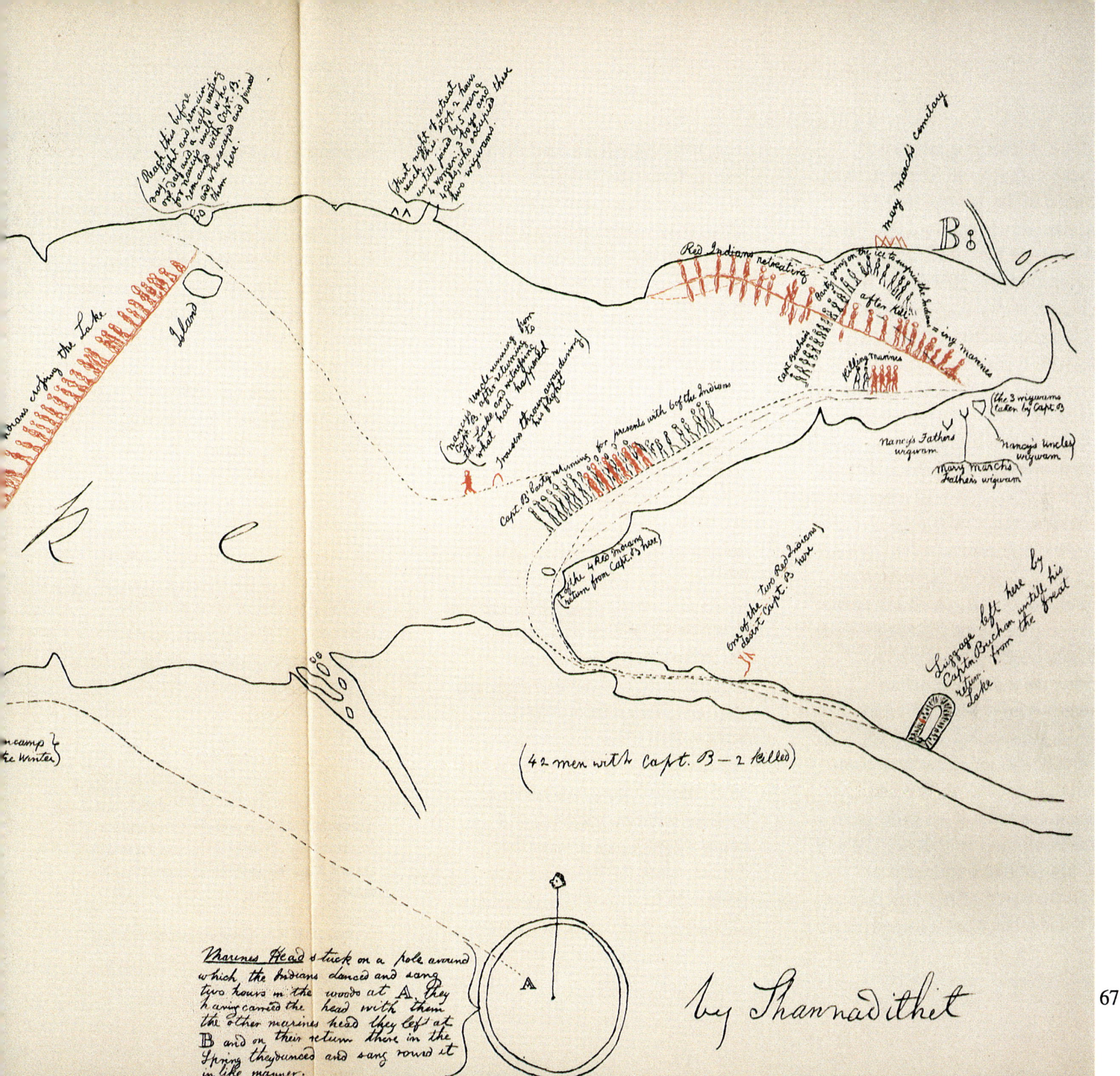

A more impressive attempt to make contact with the Beothuks occurred in the winter of 1811 when the Newfoundland governor sent Lt. David Buchan with a small force of marines, guided by William Cull, up the Exploits River to find Beothuks and begin negotiations with them. Buchan did come upon a large Beothuk camp whose occupants were too frightened and too surprised to either fight or run. Buchan spent a few friendly hours with his astonished hosts, but then decided to return down the river to retrieve the presents he had left behind. He left two of his own men behind, but on his return to the Indian camp he found his men killed and beheaded, lying on the ice. Fearing an ambush, Buchan retreated warily back down the river. A subsequent search for Beothuks a month later was completely unsuccessful. We will never know what fears prompted those Beothuks, on that cold, sleety day, almost two hundred years ago, to kill the two marines and take to the woods, but what a tragedy it was. If the Beothuks could have been taken under the protective custody of the government in 1811, they just might have been able to survive and their descendants would be living among us today.

But this was not to be, and after the Buchan expedition, the cycle of theft and murderous retaliation continued. In 1818, a group of Beothuks raided a premises at the bottom of the Bay of Exploits and cut loose a fully laden boat which belonged to John Peyton, Senior. Peyton was a local fish and fur merchant who had earned a reputation as a hard man who retaliated savagely against Indians he thought guilty of stealing from his stations. Peyton informed the governor of his loss and earlier ones as well, and received permission from the governor to try to recover what he had lost, and to bring a captive back alive. Of course, what the governor had done was to authorize a punitive expedition and this is exactly what happened. In March of 1819, the Peyton expedition reached a Beothuk settlement on Red Indian Lake and captured a woman, after killing her husband, and perhaps one other man. The woman, whose name was Demasduit (called Mary March by her captors) had been taken away from her sick child who later died. Once Peyton had been given permission to take a captive, it was almost inevitable that there would be killing. The two peoples could not speak each other's language; an attempt by whites to secure a captive understandably would result in other members of the band defending him or her. It was perhaps fortunate that Beothuk casualties were as small as they were.

An imaginative depiction by John Maunder Sr, of the capture of Demasduit (Mary March) and the killing of her husband.

Courtesy of the Mary March Regional Museum and Historic Resources Division.

William Cormack's 1822 search for the Beothuks led him across Newfoundland. Central Newfoundland's Mt. Sylvester (background) was named for Cormack's Micmac guide, Joe Sylvester.

Photo courtesy of Gerald Penney.

After her capture, Peyton deposited Demasduit with the Anglican missionary in Twillingate, the Reverend John Leigh. When it was possible to travel to St. John's she was sent there to see Governor Hamilton. Once Hamilton had learned the particulars of her capture, he sent her back to the Bay of Exploits to be reunited with her child. She was placed on board a vessel captained by a William Glascock. Glascock spent a month cruising Notre Dame Bay in a futile attempt to leave his captive with a Beothuk party. Indians were indeed sighted, but, not surprisingly, it was not possible for the whites to make contact with them. Frustrated, Glascock returned Demasduit to Twillingate where she was once again left with the Reverend Leigh.

Governor Hamilton, however, was determined to send Demasduit back to her people. To do this, Hamilton ordered Buchan, the first official to make contact with the Beothuks, to direct the return of Demasduit up the Exploits to her people's winter camp. By this point—the fall of 1819—Demasduit was seriously ill with what was probably tuberculosis, and she died on board Buchan's vessel on January 8, 1820. Although she could not be returned to her people alive, Buchan, rather unrealistically, also hoped that he could make use of an extended funeral cortege to make contact with the remnants of the Beothuks. Demasduit's body was left on the shores of Red Indian Lake. No live Beothuks were encountered.

There were no more official attempts to make contact with the Beothuks, but William Cormack, a naturalist and adventurer, did set off with a Micmac guide in 1822 to find the remaining Beothuks. Cormack wound up walking across the island from Trinity Bay to the west coast, and it is fairly clear that his guide, perhaps wiser than he, consistently led him south of Beothuk territory so as to avoid contact with the island's aborigines.

The year after Cormack's unsuccessful quest, three Beothuk women, starving and sick, surrendered to William Cull in New Bay, Notre Dame Bay. They were brought to St. John's by John Peyton Junior, the son of the elder Peyton. Since the Governor was not in St. John's, they were placed in the care of Captain Buchan. Incredibly, Buchan decided to send the three sick women back to the Bay of Exploits. After wandering the shores of the Bay, two of the women died; the third, a young woman named Shanawdithit, rowed the boat that she had been given to the Peyton household on Burnt Island. There she stayed as a servant for five years. It is quite likely that during this period her people became extinct. When, in 1827, Cormack, accompanied by three guides, a Montagnais, an Abnaki, and a Micmac, searched what had been Beothuk territory, they found only deserted wigwams and abandoned graves. Shanawdithit was almost certainly the last Beothuk.

After five years with the Peytons, Shanawdithit was spirited away at the behest of the 'Beothuk Institution', a group of influential citizens founded in 1827 for the purpose of establishing friendly relations with the Beothuks. Cor-

Memorial erected to Shanawdithit, the last known Beothuk, stands on the south side of St. John's Harbour, possibly near her burial place.

mack and other members of the Institution were of the stated opinion that it was necessary to take 'that unfortunate creature under our own immediate protection' and rescue her from 'her deplorable and dark situation.' While in St. John's, Shawnadithit provided Cormack (and us) with a wealth of information about Beothuk language and culture. In fact, much of what we know about the later culture and history of the Beothuks comes from Cormack's notes. Not the least of that information was in the form of a remarkable series of drawings that Shawnadithit made illustrating a number of facets of Beothuk life as well as a pictorial representation of the final events of her people.

Tragically, those drawings would be her last tangible legacy to the future—a future devoid of her own people forever. Shawnadithit, too, fell ill, almost certainly of tuberculosis. She died in June, 1829. Her death marked the end of an entire people—one of the most tragic forms of loss that humanity can experience. We owe it to Shanawdithit, her people, and the rest of the human species, to understand what happened to the Beothuks. The cheap, lurid explanations that portray the ancestors of today's Newfoundlanders as savage brutes who killed the Beothuks 'for fun' should no longer be sufficient. The demise of Shanawdithit's people came out of an intricate interaction of factors which included the ecology of the island and its surrounding seas, the extension of a European migratory fishery to the region, and the ultimate colonization of the island by Europeans. It was not genocide, but this, that brought about Beothuk extinction, but it was no less tragic

Female figure, drawn by Shawnadithit and described as a 'dancing woman', suggests that even during the last desperate days of the Beothuks it was possible to find some joy in their lives.

Courtesy of the Newfoundland Museum

Acknowledgements

This book could not have been written without the help of a great many field workers whose conscientious labour, often under appalling conditions, at Boyd's Cove and Inspector Island produced the most significant information upon which this work is based. I would also like to thank the people of Boyd's Cove, especially the Thoms family, Comfort Cove, Summerford, and other eastern Notre Dame communities. Without their hospitality and assistance our work would have been impossible.

I would also like to thank Laurel Doucette for her encouragement and editorial skills. The impetus to begin this book came from James Tuck; without his support and ideas the book would never have been published. Many others in the academic community have provided information and help of various kinds. I owe particular debts to Anne Hart, Laurie MacLean, Charles Martijn, Cathy Mathias, Gerald Penney, Priscilla Renouf, Peter Pope, Chesley Sanger and Ruth Whitehead.

A number of people from the Newfoundland Museum were extremely generous with their time and effort. I would especially like to thank Linda Jefferson, John Maunder and Susan Maunder. Clifford Evans of the Mary March Regional Museum was particularly willing to give me access both to the resources of his institution to his knowledge. Maps and other graphics were prepared by Anne MacLeod, Anigraph Productions, St. John's. Ken Pittman, of Red Ochre Productions, St. John's, provided the cover photograph by cinematographer Michael Jones. Jack Martin and John Bourne, University Relations, Memorial University of Newfoundland, are responsible for many of the photographs.

Financial support for the research that went into this book came from the Social Sciences and Humanities Research Council, the Department of Culture, Recreation and Youth, Government of Newfoundland and Labrador, and Memorial University of Newfoundland. Analysis of the faunal remains from Boyd's Cove was done by Stephen Cumbaa of the Zooarchaeological Identification Centre, National Museum of Natural Science.